Mastering Erlang Programming

From Basics to Expert Proficiency

Contents

Introduction

Erlang is a powerful programming language designed for building scalable and fault-tolerant systems. Created in the late 1980s by Ericsson, Erlang has since become a robust tool used by developers worldwide for telecommunications, messaging systems, and other distributed applications requiring high availability. This book is designed to take you through the foundational aspects of Erlang programming to a level where you can confidently address complex problems with elegant, concurrent solutions.

Erlang embodies a unique philosophy that emphasizes concurrency, fault tolerance, and distributed computing. These principles are not just theoretical constructs but have been proven in numerous real-world applications. Companies like WhatsApp, Klarna, and Ericsson use Erlang to handle massive numbers of concurrent connections and ensure system reliability. This language's capacity to manage faults gracefully and maintain operations makes it particularly suitable for systems where downtime is unacceptable.

Understanding Erlang involves diving into its ecosystem, which encompasses not only the language itself but also its runtime environment, standard libraries, and the OTP (Open Telecom Platform) framework. The OTP framework is a set of libraries and design principles that provide powerful building blocks for creating concurrent and distributed software systems. It abstracts many of the complexities involved in process management and supervision, allowing developers to focus on the business logic of their applications.

Erlang's syntax and semantics may initially appear unconventional compared to more mainstream languages like Python or JavaScript, but this unconventionality is a byproduct of the language's design goals. Erlang's lightweight processes and explicit message-passing model are fundamental to its ability to handle concurrency efficiently. The language uses immutable data structures and a functional programming paradigm, which together contribute to more predictable and maintainable code.

In this book, we will explore the trajectory of Erlang, from its historical origins to its contemporary applications, and delve into its key features and components. We will start with the basics, such as setting up the environment and running simple programs. As we progress, you will gain a thorough understanding of Erlang's core concepts, including its unique approach to concurrency, error handling, and fault tolerance. Furthermore, we will examine the OTP framework and how it simplifies the development of robust and maintainable systems.

Whether you are a seasoned developer looking to add Erlang to your repertoire or a newcomer seeking to understand a language that powers some of the world's most reliable systems, this book will provide a structured and comprehensive guide. By the end of this journey, you will not only be proficient in Erlang but also equipped with the knowledge to build systems that leverage its strengths to deliver high-performance, fault-tolerant solutions.

Chapter 1

Introduction to Erlang

Erlang, developed by Ericsson in the 1980s, is a programming language tailored for building scalable and fault-tolerant systems, particularly in telecommunications and messaging. This chapter provides insights into Erlang's history, its underlying philosophy, and real-world applications. We will explore its key features, the Erlang ecosystem, and make comparisons with other languages. Additionally, the chapter will guide you through the installation and setup process, culminating in running your first Erlang program.

1.1 History and Origins of Erlang

Erlang's development can be traced back to the early 1980s at Ericsson, a major Swedish telecommunications company. The primary motivation for creating Erlang was to address the unique challenges faced in the telecom industry, which required systems that were not only scalable but also capable of running continuously without interruptions. This need gave rise to a language that excels in building distributed, fault-tolerant systems.

Initially, the project was led by Joe Armstrong, Robert Virding, and Mike Williams. They were tasked with finding a more effective way to build software for telephony applications. One key requirement was to develop systems that could handle numerous simultaneous conversations – in other words, systems that exhibit a high degree of concurrency.

The team began experimenting with different programming languages and paradigms, initially exploring Prolog, a logic programming language known for its concurrent execution capabilities. However, Prolog did not meet all the criteria necessary for industrial applications, particularly in terms of performance and fault tolerance. These early explorations laid the groundwork for what would become the Erlang programming language.

Erlang gathered inspiration from various programming paradigms, integrating features from logic programming, functional programming, and concurrent programming. The language was designed to support lightweight processes, message passing, and error recovery, which are critical for building highly reliable systems.

By 1987, the team had developed a prototype and by 1991, the language was formally introduced within Ericsson. Erlang quickly proved its value and efficacy. The language was adopted in several internal projects, including the AXD301, a high-capacity ATM (Asynchronous Transfer Mode) switch, which became a commercial success.

In 1998, Ericsson made a pivotal decision to open-source Erlang. This move expanded the language's community and spurred further development. Open source Erlang is referred to as the Open Telecom Platform (OTP), which includes not only the language itself but also a wide array of libraries and tools for building robust systems. This comprehensive ecosystem offers frameworks for common patterns such as finite state machines, event handling, and network protocols.

Erlang's open-source nature allowed it to grow beyond Ericsson's domain. The language found a niche in a variety of domains requiring high concurrency and reliability, notably in finance, e-commerce, and instant messaging applications. Companies such as Klarna, WhatsApp, and Bet365 have successfully leveraged Erlang to build robust high-performance systems.

Here is a concise timeline highlighting key milestones in the history and development of Erlang:

- **1986**: Joe Armstrong, Robert Virding, and Mike Williams begin investigating new languages for telephony applications.
- **1987**: The first prototype of Erlang is created.
- **1991**: Erlang is formally introduced and utilized within Ericsson.

- **1998**: Erlang is released as open-source software.
- **1999**: The OTP (Open Telecom Platform) framework is bundled with Erlang, providing a rich set of tools and libraries.
- **2000s**: Erlang sees adoption in various industries outside telecommunications.
- **2014**: WhatsApp, with its massive messaging platform built on Erlang, is acquired by Facebook, highlighting Erlang's scalability and reliability.

The success of Erlang is not merely attributed to its technical capabilities but also to its guiding philosophy. Central tenets such as "Let it crash" encapsulate the belief that systems should be designed to expect and recover from failures gracefully. Erlang's failure recovery model involves isolated processes, each running isolated from others, thus preventing system-wide crashes.

To further illustrate how Erlang's design principles were implemented, let's explore some basic syntax and experimenting with lightweight processes.

```
-module(demo_process).
-export([start/0]).

start() ->
    Pid = spawn(fun() -> loop() end),
    Pid ! {hello, self()},
    receive
        {ok, Msg} -> io:format("Received ~p~n", [Msg])
    end.

loop() ->
    receive
        {hello, From} ->
            From ! {ok, "world"},
            loop()
    end.
```

In this example, the spawn/1 function creates a new process running the loop/0 function. The main process sends a message to this new process, which then responds accordingly. This basic code snippet highlights Erlang's lightweight process model and message-passing mechanism.

Output from running the above code will be:

```
Received "world"
```

This powerful concurrency model is a key factor in Erlang's robustness and efficiency. It allows systems to manage thousands of concurrent processes with minimal overhead, a core requirement in telecommunication systems and other high-availability applications.

Erlang's journey from an internal Ericsson project to a widely used open-source language exemplifies how industry-specific needs can drive innovative solutions with universal applicability. The language's foundations in concurrency, fault tolerance, and distributed computing continue to make it relevant in today's complex software landscape.

1.2 The Philosophy Behind Erlang

Erlang's development was driven by specific design principles tailored to the needs of telecommunication systems. Understanding these foundational principles provides insight into why Erlang's constructs are designed the way they are and highlights the problems Erlang is particularly well-suited to solve.

- **Concurrency:** Erlang was designed to handle numerous concurrent activities efficiently. Its concurrency model is built around lightweight processes, which are much less resource-intensive than operating system threads. Processes in Erlang communicate through message passing, eliminating the need for locks and other traditional concurrency control mechanisms. This approach reduces the risk of common concurrency-related bugs, such as deadlocks, and enhances the ability to build scalable applications.

```
% Simple example of creating a process in Erlang
spawn(fun() -> io:format("Hello from the new process!~n") end).
```

```
Hello from the new process!
```

- **Fault-Tolerance:** Reliability is paramount in telecommunication systems, necessitating that systems remain operational despite failures in individual components. Erlang embraces the concept of "let it crash," implying that the most efficient way to handle errors is often to let processes fail and restart them in a clean state. Supervisors monitor worker processes and restarts them when they fail, ensuring system robustness.

```
% Example supervisor definition
-module(my_supervisor).
-behaviour(supervisor).

-export([start_link/0, init/1]).

start_link() ->
    supervisor:start_link({local, ?MODULE}, ?MODULE, []).

init([]) ->
    {ok, {{one_for_one, 5, 10},
          [{worker, my_worker, [], permanent, brutal_kill, worker, [my_worker]}]}}.
```

- **Distributed Computing:** Erlang was designed to run on distributed systems from the start. Its built-in support for distributed development simplifies creating applications that span multiple nodes. Erlang processes can communicate across different nodes just as they would on a single node, providing seamless distribution.

```
% Connecting two Erlang nodes
net_adm:ping('node2@host').
```

pong

- **Hot Code Swapping:** Maintenance and upgrades often require taking systems offline, but Erlang supports changing code in a running system without stopping it. This ability to upgrade systems on the fly, or "hot code swapping," minimizes downtime and is vital for high-availability systems.

```
% Load new version of a module
l(ModuleName).
```

- **Functional Programming:** Erlang is a functional programming language, which means that functions are first-class citizens, and immutable data structures are emphasized. This immutability simplifies reasoning about program behavior, especially in concurrent systems where data races are common.

```
% Example of immutability and higher-order functions
Sum = lists:foldl(fun(X, Acc) -> X + Acc end, 0, [1, 2, 3, 4, 5]).
```

15

- **Small Footprint and Efficiency:** Erlang's runtime system is designed to have a small memory footprint and to manage resources efficiently. This efficiency makes it feasible to run millions of concurrent processes on a single machine, a crucial requirement for massive telecommunication systems.

```
% Check the memory usage of a process
process_info(self(), memory).
```

```
{memory, 23360}
```

- **Soft Real-Time Capabilities:** Telecommunication systems often have strict timing requirements. Erlang provides soft real-time capabilities, meaning it can handle a high rate of operations within predictable time constraints, though it does not guarantee hard real-time constraints.

```
% Simple timer in Erlang
timer:sleep(1000).
io:format("One second has passed.~n").
```

```
One second has passed.
```

By adhering to these principles, Erlang satisfies the stringent requirements of modern telecommunication systems, making it a powerful tool for building robust, distributed, and concurrent applications.

1.3 Real-World Use Cases for Erlang

Erlang's design, with its roots in the telecommunications industry, makes it exceptionally suitable for systems requiring high availability, concurrency, and fault tolerance. This section delves into the real-world applications of Erlang, showcasing its practicality and effectiveness across various domains.

1. Telecommunications:

Erlang's genesis is deeply entwined with the needs of the telecommunications industry. Ericsson, the company behind Erlang, needed a language to develop reliable telecommunication systems. Erlang's ability to handle multiple connections simultaneously and recover from faults gracefully makes it ideal for this sector.

One prominent example is the AXD301, an ATM switch developed by Ericsson. This system, comprising over a million lines of Erlang code, can handle thousands of transactions per second and achieve nine nines (99.9999999%) of reliability. Such robustness is critical in telecommunications, where uptime and reliability are paramount.

Code Example: Erlang in Telecommunication

```
-module(telecom).
-export([start/0, handle_call/3]).

start() ->
    {ok, Pid} = gen_server:start({local, ?MODULE}, ?MODULE, [], []),
    Pid.

handle_call({connect, User}, _From, State) ->
    io:format("Connecting user: ~p~n", [User]),
    {reply, ok, State};
handle_call({disconnect, User}, _From, State) ->
    io:format("Disconnecting user: ~p~n", [User]),
    {reply, ok, State}.

%% gen_server callbacks
init([]) ->
    {ok, []}.
```

2. Messaging Systems:

Erlang's lightweight process model and built-in support for messaging make it an excellent choice for developing messaging platforms. An exemplary case is WhatsApp, which uses Erlang to serve millions of users with minimal hardware. WhatsApp's server infrastructure, powered by Erlang, efficiently handles over 2 million connections per server.

Performance Output Example: WhatsApp-like System

```
Server is handling over 2 million active connections.
System uptime: 99.9999%
Messages processed per second: 3,000,000+
```

3. E-Commerce:

Erlang's ability to manage thousands of concurrent activities seamlessly finds applications in e-commerce platforms. For instance, Klarna, a Swedish payment service, utilizes Erlang for their backend systems. Klarna's environment processes millions of transactions, ensuring speed and reliability, attributes intrinsic to Erlang.

```
-module(payment_system).
-export([start_payment/1, process_payment/2]).

start_payment(User) ->
    spawn(fun() -> process_payment(User, ok) end).

process_payment(User, Status) ->
```

```
    io:format("Processing payment for user: ~p with status: ~p~n", [User, Status]),
    {ok, updated_status} = update_payment_status(User, Status),
    updated_status.

update_payment_status(User, CurrentStatus) ->
    %% Dummy function for updating payment status
    {ok, processed}.
```

4. Online Gaming:

The concurrent and distributed nature of Erlang makes it highly suitable for building online multiplayer games. For example, the game *Riot Games' League of Legends* uses Erlang for its chat service, managing millions of players simultaneously. Erlang's ability to manage numerous processes concurrently and recover from errors is crucial in delivering a seamless gaming experience.

5. Financial Systems:

Financial systems require both high reliability and the ability to process numerous transactions in real-time. Erlang's features align perfectly with these requisites. Companies like Goldman Sachs and Credit Suisse use Erlang for building robust trading and messaging systems, benefitting from its fault tolerance and concurrency.

```
-module(trading_system).
-export([trade/3, log_trade/2]).

trade(User, Stock, Quantity) ->
    %% Simulate trading logic
    io:format("Trading ~p shares of ~p for user: ~p~n", [Quantity, Stock, User]),
    log_trade(User, ok).

log_trade(User, Status) ->
    io:format("Logging trade for user: ~p with status: ~p~n", [User, Status]),
    {ok, logged}.
```

6. Internet of Things (IoT):

With the proliferation of IoT devices, scalable and reliable systems to handle device communication and data processing are essential. Erlang's concurrent processing model and fault tolerance are highly valuable in IoT applications. Examples include smart home systems and sensor networks where devices need to communicate and coordinate reliably.

Algorithm Example: IoT Device Coordinate

Data: Device_ID, Initial_State
Result: Coordinate IoT Device

```
Initialize device with Initial_State;
Establish connection to central hub;
while device is active do
    Send device status to hub;
    Receive control commands from hub;
    if command received then
        Process command;
        Update device state;
    else
        Maintain current state;
```

The practical applications of Erlang in various industries underscore its unique strengths in handling concurrent operations and ensuring system reliability. Each example demonstrates how Erlang's features translate to real-world benefits, making it a powerful tool for building resilient, high-performance systems.

1.4 Key Features and Benefits of Erlang

Erlang's distinctiveness lies in its robust architecture, built to optimize concurrent processing and fault tolerance. This section delves into the core features that make Erlang an exemplary choice for today's demanding computational tasks, alongside the primary benefits that these features confer.

Concurrency is central to Erlang, managed through lightweight processes that are initiated within the Erlang virtual machine (VM). Unlike traditional operating system processes, Erlang processes consume minimal memory and computational overhead.

```
% Spawning a new process in Erlang
Pid = spawn(fun() -> io:format("Hello, World!~n") end).
```

Inter-process communication (IPC) in Erlang is achieved using message passing, a method that decouples processes from one another. This results in systems with high resilience and scalability, particularly suitable for distributed systems.

Pid denotes the process identifier in Erlang. Messages are sent to processes using the following syntax:

```
% Sending a message to a process
Pid ! {message, "Hello, Erlang!"}.
```

Erlang employs pattern matching to handle these messages, ensuring precise and efficient message reception and response.

```
% Receiving a message
receive
    {message, Text} -> io:format("Received: ~s~n", [Text])
end.
```

Fault tolerance in Erlang is bolstered by its "let it crash" philosophy, which promotes the creation of supervisory structures to manage error recovery. Supervisors monitor worker processes and reboot them as needed, following a predefined strategy.

A simple supervisor definition may look like this:

```
% Supervisor definition
-module(my_supervisor).
-behaviour(supervisor).

init([]) ->
    {ok, {{one_for_one, 5, 10},
        [{worker_id, worker_module, []}]}}.

start_link() ->
    supervisor:start_link({local, ?MODULE}, ?MODULE, []).
```

Hot code swapping is another hallmark of Erlang, allowing system updates without downtime. This feature is particularly beneficial for systems requiring 24/7 availability, such as telecommunications networks and web servers.

Dynamic code replacement in Erlang can be achieved as follows:

```
% Loading new version of a module
l(my_module).

% Calling function from updated module
my_module:my_function().
```

Erlang's robust standard library and third-party libraries extend its capabilities, providing ready-made solutions for a vast array of tasks. The OTP (Open Telecom Platform) framework is replete with tools and libraries designed to support robust fault-tolerant applications.

Erlang's efficiency in handling concurrent tasks is primarily due to its lightweight process model. It leverages the BEAM (Bogdan/Björn's Erlang Abstract Machine) VM to manage these processes efficiently. The

VM handles thousands of processes with minimal context-switching overhead as compared to traditional operating systems.

The distribution capabilities of Erlang allow seamless communication between nodes in a distributed system. Each node in an Erlang system can be on a different machine, yet they can communicate as if they were processes on the same machine.

Node Communication Example:

```
% Assuming node1 and node2 are set up correctly
{ok, Pid} = rpc:call(node2@host, my_module, my_function, [Args]).
```

Erlang's immutable data structures contribute to its reliability, as immutability removes the complexities associated with state changes, leading to fewer bugs and predictable behaviours.

The following highlights the construction of an immutable list in Erlang:

```
% Constructing an immutable list
List = [1, 2, 3],
NewList = [0 | List].
```

Erlang's garbage collector is optimized for systems with numerous processes, each with its own heap. This per-process garbage collection strategy ensures minimal impact on system performance, even under heavy load.

When considering real-time applications, Erlang shines with its support for soft real-time capabilities. It guarantees that tasks are processed within a time frame, suitable for applications where timing is critical but hard real-time constraints of systems like those used in automotive control are not required.

Here's a basic example of implementing a timeout in a receive block:

```
receive
    {msg, Data} -> process(Data)
after 5000 ->
    io:format("Timeout occurred~n")
end.
```

Finally, Erlang's comprehensive tooling ecosystem, including rebar3 for build automation and observer for real-time system monitoring, enhances developer efficiency and system maintainability.

As enumerated, Erlang's unique features — concurrency, fault tolerance, hot code swapping, distribution capabilities, and more — culminate in a powerful toolkit for developing reliable, scalable, and maintainable systems.

1.5 The Erlang Ecosystem

The Erlang Ecosystem comprises a suite of tools, libraries, and frameworks that complement the core Erlang programming language. This ecosystem facilitates the development of robust, scalable, and fault-tolerant applications. Understanding the ecosystem is crucial for leveraging Erlang's full potential in both development and production environments.

1. Erlang/OTP (Open Telecom Platform)

The cornerstone of the Erlang ecosystem is Erlang/OTP. OTP is a collection of libraries and design principles crucial for building concurrent and distributed applications. At the heart of OTP are:

- Supervision Trees: These structures are fundamental to building fault-tolerant applications. A supervision tree comprises a set of processes, one of which (the supervisor) manages the others, restarting them if they fail.
- GenServer: This generic server behavior abstracts the creation, management, and communication between processes. Utilizing GenServer streamlines the development of server processes that maintain state, handle requests, and perform tasks asynchronously.
- Applications: In OTP, applications represent a packaged collection of modules, processes, and configuration files that together provide a specific functionality. They form the modular units of an Erlang-based system, making it easier to manage dependencies and upgrades.

2. BEAM Virtual Machine

Erlang applications run on the BEAM (Bogdan/Björn's Erlang Abstract Machine) virtual machine. The BEAM VM is designed to support large-scale concurrent systems, featuring lightweight process management, efficient garbage collection, and robust message passing. These attributes ensure high performance and reliability, even under heavy loads.

3. EDoc

EDoc is the primary tool for automating the documentation of Erlang code. It extracts documentation directly from source code comments, formatted in a specific manner to produce comprehensive HTML pages. Proper documentation is essential for maintaining and scaling large projects, and EDoc standardizes this process.

```
%%% A basic example of EDoc documentation in Erlang

-module(example).
-author("Author Name").

%% @doc
%% This function calculates the sum of two numbers.
%%
%% @spec sum(integer(), integer()) -> integer().
sum(A, B) ->
    A + B.
```

4. Dialyzer

Dialyzer (DIscrepancy AnaLYZer for ERlang programs) is a static analysis tool that identifies software discrepancies such as type errors, unreachable code, and unnecessary tests. Unlike traditional type checkers, Dialyzer adopts a "success typing" approach, ensuring it only identifies bugs without generating false negatives.

Dialyzer can be integrated into the development workflow to enhance code quality:

```
$ dialyzer --build_plt --apps erts kernel stdlib
$ dialyzer example.erl
```

5. Common Test

Common Test is a robust framework for automated testing of Erlang applications. Test cases in Common Test are written as Erlang modules and can be organized into suites. It supports test case groupings, parallel test execution, and provides detailed logs for analysis.

```
%%% A simple test suite in Common Test

-module(example_SUITE).
-include_lib("common_test/include/ct.hrl").

%%
%% This callback function initializes the test suite data.
%%
init_per_suite(Config) ->
    {ok, Config}.

%%
%% This is a sample test case.
%%
test_sum(Config) ->
    Result = example:sum(2, 3),
    ?assertEqual(5, Result).
```

6. Rebar3

Rebar3 is a build tool that simplifies the management of Erlang projects. It supports dependency management, compilation, testing, and release handling. Rebar3 configuration is managed through a `rebar.config` file, specifying dependencies and plugins.

```
%%% A sample rebar.config file

{erl_opts, [debug_info]}.

{deps, [
    {cowboy, "2.8.0"}
]}.
```

Using Rebar3 streamlines project setup and ensures consistency across development environments:

```
$ rebar3 compile
$ rebar3 ct
```

7. Mnesia

Mnesia is a distributed database management system integrated into the Erlang/OTP framework. It offers both real-time and transactional capabilities, making it ideal for applications requiring high availability and fault tolerance. Mnesia supports complex data types and automatic distribution across nodes:

```
%%% Basic Mnesia example

%% Create a new table
mnesia:create_table(person, [{attributes, record_info(fields, person)}]),

%% Insert a record
mnesia:transaction(fun() -> mnesia:write(#person{id = 1, name = "Alice"}) end).
```

8. Observer

Observer is a graphical tool for monitoring and inspecting the state of an Erlang system. It provides insights into process performance, system load, memory utilization, and communication patterns. Observer is invaluable for debugging and performance tuning.

To access Observer, run the following command in the Erlang shell:

```
1> observer:start().
```

9. Hex and Hex.pm

Hex is the package manager for the Erlang ecosystem, and Hex.pm is its repository. Similar to package managers in other programming languages, Hex allows developers to publish, share, and manage libraries and dependencies. Integration with Rebar3 ensures seamless dependency resolution.

10. Elixir Interoperability

Elixir, a language built on the Erlang VM, is fully interoperable with Erlang. This interoperability allows developers to leverage the strengths of both languages within a single system. Resources such as libraries and tools in the Elixir ecosystem can be utilized in Erlang projects and vice versa.

The synergy between Erlang's robust concurrency model and Elixir's modern syntax and tooling offers a powerful combination for developing scalable, maintainable applications.

Understanding and utilizing the Erlang ecosystem effectively can significantly enhance the development process, providing tools and frameworks essential for building complex, distributed, and fault-tolerant systems.

1.6 Comparing Erlang to Other Languages

Erlang stands out in the landscape of programming languages due to its unique features tailored for building concurrent, distributed, fault-tolerant systems. To appreciate its distinctiveness, it is instructive to compare it with other languages across several dimensions: concurrency, fault tolerance, scalability, syntax, and ecosystem support.

Concurrency: Unlike many programming languages that rely on threading models for concurrent operations, Erlang employs a lightweight process model. Each Erlang process is encapsulated, with its own memory and run-time environment. This model is built into the language itself, enabling millions of processes to run concurrently without the overhead associated with operating system threads. Consider the following Erlang code snippet that spawns ten thousand processes:

```
create_processes(0) -> ok;
create_processes(N) ->
    spawn(fun() -> receive after infinity -> ok end end),
    create_processes(N-1).
```

Contrast this with typical thread management in Java, which handles concurrency using the Thread class and often requires complex synchronization primitives:

```
public class ThreadExample {
    public static void main(String[] args) {
        for (int i = 0; i < 10000; i++) {
            new Thread(() -> {
                try {
                    Thread.sleep(Long.MAX_VALUE);
                } catch (InterruptedException e) {
                    e.printStackTrace();
                }
            }).start();
        }
    }
}
```

Erlang's approach to concurrency is more efficient and simplifies the design of concurrent systems, avoiding common pitfalls encountered with thread-based models such as deadlock and race conditions.

Fault Tolerance: Erlang's 'let it crash' philosophy underpins its robust fault-tolerance mechanisms. Processes are designed to fail without harming the whole system. Supervisors are employed to monitor worker processes and take defined corrective actions when a failure occurs. Below is an illustration of a basic supervisor in Erlang:

```
-module(simple_sup).
-behaviour(supervisor).

init([]) ->
    {ok, { {one_for_one, 5, 10},
          [{worker, {my_worker, start_link, []}, permanent, brutal_kill, worker, [
                my_worker]}]
      }}.
```

Comparatively, languages such as C++ or Python lack built-in mechanisms for such fail-safe operation and often require additional libraries or frameworks to achieve similar fault tolerance.

Scalability: Erlang's inherent support for distributed computing allows it to scale seamlessly across multiple nodes. The language provides distributed capabilities out of the box; processes can communicate over a network as easily as they communicate within a single node. Here, a simple message-passing example demonstrates how processes can send messages to each other, even in a distributed setup:

```
% Node1
spawn(node2@hostname, fun() -> io:format("Hello from ~p~n", [self()]) end).

% Node2
receive
    Msg -> io:format("Received: ~p~n", [Msg])
end.
```

In comparison, achieving similar distributed capabilities in languages like Python often requires the integration of external packages such as ‘ZeroMQ‘ or ‘Pyro4‘, adding complexity and potential points of failure:

```
import zerorpc

# Server on Node1
class HelloRPC(object):
    def hello(self, name):
        return "Hello, %s" % name

s = zerorpc.Server(HelloRPC())
s.bind("tcp://0.0.0.0:4242")
s.run()

# Client on Node2
c = zerorpc.Client()
c.connect("tcp://node1hostname:4242")
print(c.hello("world"))
```

Syntax and Semantics: Erlang's syntax is designed to support its concurrency and fault-tolerant paradigms. Its syntax is declarative and concise, explicitly favoring readability in concurrent contexts. For instance, listing key-value structures using records is straightforward:

```
-record(person, {name, age}).

create_person(Name, Age) ->
    #person{name=Name, age=Age}.
```

In contrast, languages like C++ have more intricate syntax structures and significantly steeper learning curves:

```
struct Person {
    std::string name;
    int age;
};

Person createPerson(const std::string& name, int age) {
    return {name, age};
}
```

Ecosystem Support: Erlang benefits from a robust ecosystem that includes tools like OTP (Open Telecom Platform) for building complex systems. OTP provides libraries and design principles for building fault-tolerant software, offering an advantage over other languages that may require third-party frameworks. Systems such as **Apache CouchDB** and **RabbitMQ** showcase the practical application of the Erlang ecosystem, attesting to its industrial strength.

When compared with modern languages like Go (Golang), Erlang's actor-based model provides a matured concurrency mechanism, whereas Go uses goroutines and channels. The simplicity and power of Erlang's lightweight processes often surpass Go's goroutines in scenarios requiring granular fault isolation and massive parallelism.

These comparisons highlight Erlang's unique strengths, particularly for telecommunication and messaging systems demanding concurrent and resilient operations. Its language features, coupled with a mature ecosystem, make it a powerful tool for developers working in these domains. Understanding the distinctions between Erlang and other languages underscores why it remains a preferred choice for high-availability, distributed applications.

1.7 Installing and Setting Up Erlang

Prerequisites

Before installing Erlang, ensure your system satisfies the minimum requirements. The essential prerequisites include a modern operating system (OSX, Linux, or Windows) and administrative privileges for installation tasks. Additionally, we recommend updating your system to the latest stable version to avoid compatibility issues.

Downloading and Installing Erlang

The official Erlang distribution, maintained by the OTP team at Ericsson, is available from the Erlang website. The installation process varies slightly depending on the operating system.

On Unix-based Systems (Linux and macOS)

For Unix-based systems, the package manager simplifies installation. Here are the steps for Ubuntu (a Debian-based Linux distribution) and Homebrew (a package manager for macOS).

- For Ubuntu:

  ```
  sudo apt-get update
  sudo apt-get install erlang
  ```

  Once the process completes, verify the installation:

  ```
  erl -version
  ```

  Expected output:

```
Erlang/OTP 24 [erts-12.0.3] ...
```

- For macOS:

```
brew update
brew install erlang
```

Verify the installation:

```
erl -version
```

Expected output:

```
Erlang/OTP 24 [erts-12.0.3] ...
```

On Windows

For Windows, the installation uses a straightforward executable from the official Erlang website. Follow these steps:

- Download the Windows installer from the Erlang website.
- Run the installer and follow the on-screen instructions.
  - Ensure to set the destination folder path during installation.
  - Add Erlang to the system '

Verify the installation by opening a command prompt and executing:

```
erl -version
```

Expected output:

```
Erlang/OTP 24 [erts-12.0.3] ...
```

Verifying the Installation

Regardless of the platform, once Erlang is installed, verify it by starting the Erlang shell. The shell is an interactive command-line tool where Erlang code snippets can be directly executed.

Open your terminal (or command prompt on Windows) and enter:

```
erl
```

You should see something similar to:

```
Eshell V12.0.3 (abort with ^G)
1>
```

This prompt (1>) indicates that the Erlang shell is active and ready for commands.

For a functional test, input a simple arithmetic operation:

```
1> 2 + 3.
```

Expected output:

```
5
```

You can exit the shell using:

```
1> q().
```

Configuring the Environment

The Erlang environment can be customized to enhance your development workflow. Key configurations include setting environment variables and integrating Erlang with popular development tools.

Environment Variables

Ensure Erlang's executable paths are correctly set. On Unix-based systems, add the following lines to your shell profile file (7.bashrc or 7.zshrc):

```
export PATH="/usr/local/lib/erlang/bin:$PATH"
```

On Windows, ensure the installation path (e.g., C:\Program Files\Erlang\bin) is included in the $PATH environment variable. Use the system properties and environment variables dialog to adjust settings.

Integration with IDEs and Editors

Popular Integrated Development Environments (IDEs) like IntelliJ IDEA, Visual Studio Code, and Emacs support Erlang development through plugins.

- **Visual Studio Code**: Install the Erlang extension from the marketplace. - **IntelliJ IDEA**: Use the Erlang plugin from the JetBrains repository. - **Emacs**: Integrate with the erlware-mode package for syntax highlighting and shell access.

These plugins offer features such as code completion, debugging, and integrated REPL (Read-Eval-Print Loop).

Updating Erlang

Regular updates ensure that your development environment benefits from the latest features and security fixes. Updating Erlang on Unix-based systems utilizes the package manager, which simplifies version management. Regularly run:

```
sudo apt-get update
sudo apt-get upgrade erlang
```

Similarly, on macOS, execute:

```
brew update
brew upgrade erlang
```

For Windows, download the latest installer from the Erlang website and follow the installation steps again.

Throughout this process, ensure that the new version is correctly identified by running erl -version after each update. This ensures your development environment remains stable and up-to-date.

1.8 First Steps: Running Your First Erlang Program

Erlang is a uniquely powerful language designed for building concurrent, distributed, and fault-tolerant systems. In this section, we will guide you through the essential steps to create, compile, and run your first Erlang program. This hands-on approach will build a practical foundation, crucial for navigating more advanced concepts.

To begin, ensure you have Erlang installed on your system. You can verify the installation by opening a terminal and typing:

```
erl
```

You should see the Erlang shell prompt, which looks something like this:

```
Eshell V10.5.1  (abort with ^G)
1>
```

If the shell starts without any issues, you are ready to write your first Erlang program. Using your preferred text editor, create a new file named hello.erl. Erlang source files have the .erl extension. In this file, we will write a simple module that defines a function to print "Hello, World!".

```
-module(hello).
-export([hello_world/0]).

hello_world() ->
    io:format("Hello, World!~n").
```

In this program, -module(hello). declares the name of the module as hello. The -export([hello_world/0]). line specifies that the hello_world function is accessible outside this module. It takes zero arguments, as indicated by the /0. The function hello_world uses the io:format/2 function to print the string "Hello, World!" followed by a newline character (ñ).

To compile the module, open the Erlang shell and navigate to the directory containing hello.erl. Use the c() function to compile it:

```
1> c(hello).
```

If successful, you will see:

```
{ok,hello}
```

This indicates that the compilation was successful, and an object code file, hello.beam, has been created. Now you can invoke the hello_world/0 function from the Erlang shell:

```
2> hello:hello_world().
```

The expected output is:

```
Hello, World!
ok
```

The ok returned by the shell indicates that the function call completed successfully. This simple introduction covers the fundamental workflow of writing, compiling, and running an Erlang program.

For more practice, let us extend the module with a new function that accepts an argument and prints a personalized greeting. Modify hello.erl to include:

```
-module(hello).
-export([hello_world/0, greet/1]).

hello_world() ->
    io:format("Hello, World!~n").
```

```
greet(Name) ->
    io:format("Hello, ~s!~n", [Name]).
```

Here, greet/1 takes one argument, Name, and uses the s̃ control sequence to insert the string into the output. Recompile the module in the Erlang shell:

```
3> c(hello).
```

Invoke the new function with a string argument:

```
4> hello:greet("Alice").
```

The output will be:

```
Hello, Alice!
ok
```

You have now learned how to define and export functions, handle string formatting, and work with function parameters in Erlang. This sets the stage for more complex programming tasks and exposes you to the language's concise and functional syntax.

Chapter 2

Getting Started with Erlang

This chapter covers the initial steps for working with Erlang, including installing the Erlang/OTP platform and familiarizing yourself with the Erlang shell. It introduces basic syntax and semantics, variables and data types, defining functions, and compiling modules. Additionally, it provides guidance on running Erlang programs and using available documentation to support your learning journey.

2.1 Installing Erlang/OTP

To start working with Erlang, it's essential to have the Erlang/OTP (Open Telecom Platform) installed on your system. The following section details the installation process across various platforms including Windows, macOS, and Linux. This guide is designed to ensure a smooth setup, enabling you to start coding in Erlang efficiently.

Windows Installation

- Download the Erlang/OTP installer executable from the official Erlang website: https://www.erlang.org/downloads.
- Execute the downloaded file and follow the steps of the Installation Wizard.

- During the installation process, ensure that the option to add Erlang to your system's PATH is checked. This setting simplifies invoking the Erlang shell from the command line.
- To verify the installation, open the Command Prompt and execute the following command:

```
erl
```

The expected output should be similar to the below:

```
Erlang/OTP 23 [erts-11.2] [source] [64-bit] [smp:2:2] ...
Eshell V11.2  (abort with ^G)
1>
```

macOS Installation

- Ensure you have Homebrew installed. Homebrew is a package manager for macOS, which simplifies the installation of software.
- Open the Terminal and update Homebrew by running:

```
brew update
```

3. Install Erlang/OTP using Homebrew:

```
brew install erlang
```

4. To confirm the installation, start the Erlang shell by typing:

```
erl
```

The following output should appear if the installation is successful:

```
Erlang/OTP 23 [erts-11.2.1] [source] [64-bit] [smp:2:2] ...
Eshell V11.2.1  (abort with ^G)
1>
```

Linux Installation

The installation steps differ slightly depending on your Linux distribution.

Ubuntu/Debian-based systems:

1. Start by updating your package list:

```
sudo apt-get update
```

2. Install Erlang/OTP:

```
sudo apt-get install erlang
```

3. Confirm the installation was successful by starting the Erlang shell:

```
erl
```

You should observe an output similar to this:

```
Erlang/OTP 23 [erts-11.2] [source] [64-bit] [smp:2:2] ...
Eshell V11.2  (abort with ^G)
1>
```

Fedora-based systems:

1. Update your package lists:

```
sudo dnf update
```

2. Install Erlang/OTP:

```
sudo dnf install erlang
```

3. Ensure the installation by typing:

```
erl
```

The expected shell output should be:

```
Erlang/OTP 23 [erts-11.2] [source] [64-bit] [smp:2:2] ...
Eshell V11.2  (abort with ^G)
1>
```

Verifying the Installation

Regardless of the operating system, after running erl, you should see the Erlang shell ready for commands, confirming that Erlang/OTP is properly installed. If there are any errors during the initial shell start-up, revisit the installation steps to ensure each instruction was followed accurately.

Additionally, it is recommended to check the version of Erlang/OTP installed using:

```
erl -version
```

This command should output the version of Erlang/OTP in use. Ensuring the correct version aligns with the intended Erlang programming features you plan to use is essential.

Environment Configuration

After installation, you might need to configure your environment to streamline your development workflow further. This configuration includes setting environment variables and modifying the system's PATH if not done automatically:

- **Windows**: Modify the system's PATH environment variable to include the directory where Erlang is installed.
- **macOS**: Homebrew typically manages path settings automatically.
- **Linux**: Check and export the necessary paths in your shell configuration files such as ~/.bashrc or ~/.bash_profile for bash, or equivalent for other shells.

For instance, adding the following line to ~/.bashrc ensures that the Erlang executables are found by the shell:

```
export PATH=$PATH:/usr/local/lib/erlang/bin
```

After making changes to the configuration files, make sure to reload them using:

```
source ~/.bashrc
```

All these steps ensure that your development environment is well-prepared. It allows you to invoke the Erlang shell and other related commands seamlessly, facilitating a smoother coding experience.

2.2 Erlang Shell Basics

The Erlang shell is an interactive command-line interface that provides a powerful environment for developing, testing, and debugging Erlang code. Upon starting the shell, you are greeted with the Erlang prompt, signified by the number 1>. This prompt indicates that the shell is ready to accept Erlang expressions. Each input expression is evaluated, and the result is displayed along with the next prompt, incremented by one.

To start the Erlang shell, navigate to your terminal and type:

```
$ erl
```

This command initializes the shell, and you will see something similar to the following:

```
Erlang/OTP 24 [erts-11.2] [source] [...]

Eshell V11.2  (abort with ^G)
1>
```

In this session, we explore fundamental operations and commands to harness the capabilities of the Erlang shell effectively.

Arithmetic Operations

You can perform basic arithmetic operations within the shell. To add, subtract, multiply, or divide numbers, you simply input the expression as you would in typical mathematical notation:

```
1> 5 + 3.
2> 10 - 4.
3> 7 * 6.
4> 20 / 5.
```

The output of these expressions will be displayed below the prompts:

```
1> 5 + 3.
8
2> 10 - 4.
6
3> 7 * 6.
42
4> 20 / 5.
4.0
```

Note that the division operation yields a floating-point number even if both operands are integers.

Variables

In Erlang, variables are assigned using the = operator. Once assigned, the value of a variable cannot be changed, adhering to the functional programming paradigm's immutability principle. Let's demonstrate variable assignment in the shell:

```
1> X = 10.
2> Y = X + 5.
3> Z = X * Y.
```

Upon execution, the shell will display:

```
1> X = 10.
10
2> Y = X + 5.
15
3> Z = X * Y.
150
```

Trying to reassign a value to an already bound variable will result in an error:

```
4> X = 20.
```

The output will indicate a badmatch error as follows:

```
** exception error: no match of right hand side value 20
```

Functions

Functions are one of the core components of Erlang. You can define and invoke anonymous functions directly within the shell. An anonymous function is defined using the fun keyword. For instance:

```
1> Double = fun(X) -> 2 * X end.
2> Double(8).
```

The results will be:

```
1> Double = fun(X) -> 2 * X end.
#Fun<erl_eval.6.128620087>
2> Double(8).
16
```

You can also define recursive functions by invoking fun inside its own body. For example, a factorial function:

```
3> Factorial = fun(0) -> 1; (N) -> N * eval(Factorial(N - 1)) end.
4> Factorial(5).
```

The shell will evaluate the recursive function as follows:

```
3> Factorial = fun(0) -> 1; (N) -> N * eval(Factorial(N - 1)) end.
#Fun<erl_eval.6.128620087>
4> Factorial(5).
120
```

Module Loading and Compilation

While the shell is convenient for quick tests and experiments, developing larger applications will necessitate compiling and loading Erlang modules. For instance, consider a module math_ops.erl containing basic arithmetic functions. Suppose this file is located in the current directory:

```
-module(math_ops).
-export([add/2, subtract/2, multiply/2, divide/2]).

add(X, Y) -> X + Y.
subtract(X, Y) -> X - Y.
multiply(X, Y) -> X * Y.
divide(X, Y) -> X / Y.
```

To compile and load this module in the Erlang shell, use the c/1 function:

```
1> c(math_ops).
```

The shell will output:

```
{ok,math_ops}
```

After successful compilation, you can invoke the module's functions:

```
2> math_ops:add(5,3).
```

The result will be:

```
2> math_ops:add(5, 3).
8
```

Shell Commands

Several built-in shell commands help manage and navigate your session:

- b() - Prints all bound variables and their values.
- f() - Clears all variable bindings.
- f(Var) - Clears the binding of a specific variable.
- h() - Prints the command history.
- q() - Exits the shell.

For example:

```
3> b().
```

This will output all currently bound variables:

```
X = 10
Y = 15
Z = 150
```

These features make the Erlang shell an invaluable tool for both learning the language and conducting rapid development and testing.

2.3 Basic Syntax and Semantics

Erlang, being a functional programming language, has a distinct approach to syntax and semantics compared to imperative languages. Understanding these foundational elements is crucial for mastering the language and writing efficient programs.

Atoms are constants whose value is their own name. They are mostly used to denote distinct values. Atoms start with a lowercase letter or are enclosed in single quotes if they contain non-alphanumeric characters or start with an uppercase letter.

```
atom1.
'Atom-2'.
```

Variables in Erlang names must begin with an uppercase letter or an underscore. Once a variable is bound to a value, it cannot be changed, enforcing immutability.

```
A = 10.
Hello = "world".
```

Tuples are fixed-size collections of values, which can be heterogeneous. They are enclosed in curly braces.

```
{atom, 123, "string"}.
```

Lists are dynamic-length collections which can also be heterogeneous. They are enclosed in square brackets. List concatenation is performed using the double vertical bar operator (|).

```
[1, 2, 3].
["foo", "bar"].
[1, 2] ++ [3, 4]. % Results in [1, 2, 3, 4]
```

Strings in Erlang are lists of integers where each number represents the ASCII value of a character.

```
"hello" == [104, 101, 108, 108, 111]. % Evaluates to true
```

Pattern Matching is a fundamental concept, providing a robust way to destructure data. The '=' operator in Erlang is a match operator, not an assignment operator.

```
{X, Y} = {1, 2}. % X becomes 1 and Y becomes 2

X = 3,
case X of
    1 -> "one";
    2 -> "two";
    3 -> "three"
end.

\begin{FittedVerbatim}
"three"
\end{FittedVerbatim}

\textbf{\textit{Functions}} in Erlang are first-class citizens. Syntax for defining
    functions in Erlang is straightforward: A function definition is made up of one or
    more clauses, separated by semicolons, each consisting of a head and a body.

\begin{lstlisting}
factorial(0) -> 1;
factorial(N) when N > 0 -> N * factorial(N - 1).
```

This recursive definition computes the factorial of a number, leveraging pattern matching and guards for input validation.

Guards provide additional checks in function clauses or cases, ensuring conditions are met before clause execution.

```
absolute_value(X) when X >= 0 -> X;
absolute_value(X) when X < 0 -> -X.
```

Here, when $X >= 0$ and when $X < 0$ are guards, ensuring that absolute_value(-5) evaluates to 5.

Modules encapsulate related functions, providing a means for code organization and reuse. A module starts with the -module() attribute and typically has a -export() attribute to specify the public interface.

```
-module(math).
-export([add/2, subtract/2]).

add(A, B) -> A + B.
subtract(A, B) -> A - B.
```

In this example, math is a module that provides two arithmetic functions: add/2 and subtract/2. The numbers after the function names in the -export() attribute indicate arity, the number of arguments the function takes.

Comments are essential for code documentation and can be single-line or multi-line. Single-line comments start with the % character, while multi-line comments are enclosed in %%- -%%%.

```
\% This is a single-line comment

%\{
This is a
multi-line
comment
\%\}
```

Control Structures such as if, case, and receive are also part of Erlang's syntax. They enable conditional execution of code blocks.

```
if
    X > 0 -> positive;
    X == 0 -> zero;
    X < 0 -> negative
end.
```

```
case Expression of
    Pattern1 -> actions1;
    Pattern2 -> actions2;
    _ -> other_actions
end.
```

Lastly, the receive block is unique to Erlang, facilitating concurrency by handling messages sent to a process.

```
receive
    {msg, Content} -> io:format("Received: ~p~n", [Content]);
    after 5000 -> timeout
end.
```

This block waits for a message in the form of $\{msg, Content\}$, printing its content, or times out after 5000 milliseconds if no message is received.

Understanding these basic syntax and semantics elements is pivotal to utilizing Erlang's full potential. These fundamentals lay the groundwork for more advanced topics such as concurrent programming and fault-tolerant systems development.

2.4 Variables and Data Types

Erlang provides an expressive set of features for handling variables and various data types. Understanding the details of how variables and data types work is crucial for writing effective and efficient Erlang code.

Variables in Erlang are single-assignment, meaning once they are bound to a value, they cannot be reassigned. Variable names must start with an uppercase letter or an underscore (_), followed by any combination of letters, digits, and underscores.

```
VariableName = 10.
Another_Variable = "Hello, Erlang!".
```

Attempting to reassign the value of a variable will result in an error:

```
VariableName = 20. % This would cause an error since VariableName is already bound
    to 10.
```

Erlang supports a variety of data types, including integers, floats, atoms, tuples, lists, and more. Each data type serves a different purpose and has unique characteristics.

Integers and Floats

Integers in Erlang are arbitrary-precision, which means they can be of any size limited only by the memory of the system. Floats are represented using double-precision floating point numbers.

```
IntegerVar = 42.
FloatVar = 3.14.
```

Atoms

Atoms are constants whose value is their own name. They are used frequently in Erlang for enumeration and pattern matching.

```
AtomVar = hello.
AnotherAtom = 'An atom with spaces'. % Atoms can include spaces if enclosed in
    single quotes.
```

Tuples

Tuples are fixed-size collections of values. They are used to group multiple values together. Tuples are expressed within curly braces {}.

```
TupleVar = {ok, "This is a tuple", 123}.
```

The elements of a tuple can be of any type, and they can be accessed using pattern matching.

```
{Status, Message, Number} = TupleVar.
```

Lists

Lists are dynamically-sized collections of values. They are one of the most versatile and commonly used data structures in Erlang. Lists are expressed within square brackets

.

```
ListVar = [1, 2, 3, 4, 5].
```

Lists can be concatenated using the ++ operator and can be split using the – operator:

```
ConcatenatedList = ListVar ++ [6, 7, 8].
SplitList = ListVar -- [2, 4].
```

You can also pattern match on lists to extract their head and tail:

```
[Head | Tail] = ListVar. % Head will be bound to 1, Tail will be [2, 3, 4, 5].
```

Strings

Strings in Erlang are actually lists of integers where each integer represents a character's ASCII value. Despite this, strings are handled with a special syntax:

```
StringVar = "Hello, World!".
```

Binaries

Binaries are used for handling large amounts of raw byte data. They are expressed using the «» syntax.

```
BinaryVar = <<1, 2, 3, 4>>.
```

Binaries can be pattern matched similarly to lists and tuples:

```
<<A, B, Rest/binary>> = BinaryVar.
```

Maps

Maps are key-value collections available in Erlang starting from version 17. They are expressed using the #{} syntax.

```
MapVar = #{"name" => "Alice", "age" => 30}.
```

Values associated with specific keys in a map can be accessed and updated as follows:

```
Name = MapVar#{"name"}.
UpdatedMapVar = MapVar#{"age" := 31}.
```

Records

Records are another way of grouping related values. They are similar to structs in other programming languages. Records must be defined with a -record directive in modules.

```
-record(person, {name, age}).
PersonVar = #person{name = "Bob", age = 25}.
```

Values in a record can be accessed and updated via pattern matching:

```
#person{name = PersonName, age = PersonAge} = PersonVar.
UpdatedPersonVar = PersonVar#person{age = 26}.
```

Understanding and properly using these variable types will significantly enhance your ability to write sophisticated Erlang programs. Proper selection of data types should consider the specific requirements and constraints of your application.

2.5 Defining Functions

In Erlang, functions are fundamental building blocks used to encapsulate sequences of expressions into reusable units. Erlang supports both named functions, within modules, and anonymous functions. This section delves into the syntax and semantics of defining these functions, elucidating their usage through practical examples.

Named functions are defined within modules using the fun keyword, and they must be compiled before use.

```
-module(math).
-export([add/2, subtract/2]).

add(X, Y) ->
    X + Y.

subtract(X, Y) ->
    X - Y.
```

In the above example:

- -module(math). declares the module name as math.
- -export([add/2, subtract/2]). indicates that the functions add/2 and subtract/2 are accessible from outside the module. The /2 denotes that the functions take two arguments.
- add(X, Y) -> X + Y. and subtract(X, Y) -> X - Y. are function definitions where X and Y are parameters.

Compilation ensures that the syntax is correct and the functions are converted into bytecode for execution. To compile, save the file as math.erl and run the following commands in the Erlang shell:

```
1> c(math).
{ok,math}
```

The output ok,math signifies that the module has been successfully compiled. You can now use the functions:

```
2> math:add(10, 5).
15
3> math:subtract(10, 5).
5
```

The first command calls the add function with 10 and 5 as arguments, returning 15. The second command calls the subtract function, returning 5.

Erlang also supports pattern matching in function definitions. This allows functions to behave differently based on the structure and values of their arguments.

```
factorial(0) ->
    1;
factorial(N) when N > 0 ->
    N * factorial(N - 1).
```

In the factorial function:

- `factorial(0) -> 1;` matches when the argument is 0 and returns 1.
- `factorial(N) when N > 0 -> N * factorial(N - 1).` uses a guard clause `when N > 0` to ensure N is positive and implements the recursive case of the factorial function.

To use this function, define it in a module, compile, and execute:

```
-module(math_ext).
-export([factorial/1]).

factorial(0) ->
    1;
factorial(N) when N > 0 ->
    N * factorial(N - 1).
```

After compiling with `c(math_ext).`, use it as follows:

```
4> math_ext:factorial(5).
120
```

Anonymous functions are defined using the `fun` keyword and can be assigned to variables.

```
F = fun(X, Y) -> X + Y end.
```

You can invoke them by referencing the variable:

```
5> F(10, 5).
15
```

Combining named and anonymous functions promotes flexible and powerful code reuse. Understanding and leveraging these constructs is vital for mastering Erlang programming. Implementing robust functions with pattern matching and recursion enriches problem-solving strategies in concurrent applications.

2.6 Modules and Compilation

Erlang programs are structured in units called modules. A module in Erlang is essentially a file containing a collection of related functions.

Each module typically represents a distinct part of the application's functionality, which promotes better organization and design. To define a module, we use the -module attribute followed by the module's name.

Here's a simple example of an Erlang module:

```
-module(math_ops).
-export([add/2, subtract/2]).

add(X, Y) ->
    X + Y.

subtract(X, Y) ->
    X - Y.
```

In this example, the module is named math_ops. The -export attribute specifies the functions available for external use. Each function is identified by its name and arity (the number of arguments it takes), denoted as function/arity. For instance, the add/2 function takes two arguments.

2.7 Compilation

Once a module has been defined, it must be compiled before it can be used. To compile a module, follow these steps:

- Save the module with a .erl file extension. In the above example, the file should be saved as math_ops.erl.
- Open the Erlang shell.
- Use the c/1 function to compile the module.

Within the Erlang shell, the compilation process looks like this:

```
1> c(math_ops).
{ok,math_ops}
```

{ok,math_ops}

If there are no syntax errors in the source file, Erlang will produce a .beam file, which is the compiled version of the module. In the example above, the generated file is math_ops.beam. The feedback from the shell, {ok,math_ops}, confirms that the compilation has succeeded.

2.8 Using Compiled Modules

After successful compilation, the functions within the module can be called from the Erlang shell or other modules:

```
2> math_ops:add(10, 5).
15

3> math_ops:subtract(10, 5).
5
```

```
15
5
```

The general form of calling a function in a module is ModuleName:FunctionName(Arguments...).

2.9 Error Handling in Compilation

Should there be an error during the compilation process, the compiler will provide diagnostic messages indicating the nature and location of the error. Here's an example of an error message you might encounter:

```
1> c(math_ops).
math_ops.erl:6: syntax error before: '->'
error
```

In this case, the error message indicates there's a syntax error before the -> symbol on line 6 of math_ops.erl. It is imperative to carefully review and correct the source code based on the diagnostic information provided by the compiler.

2.10 Module Attributes

Modules can include several attributes, but two of the most commonly used are -module and -export. Additional attributes such as -import, -define, and -behaviour cater to more advanced features but follow a similar declarative format.

The -import attribute allows you to use functions from other modules without prefixing them with the module name, which can streamline code if numerous functions from the same module are being utilized.

```
-import(lists, [map/2, foldl/3]).
```

In this example, the map/2 and foldl/3 functions from the lists module are imported.

The -define attribute is used to create macros, which can simplify repetitive or complex expressions.

```
-define(TEN, 10).

multiply_by_ten(X) ->
    X * ?TEN.
```

Here, ?TEN is a macro that expands to 10. Macros are useful for code clarity and maintenance, especially when constants or frequently used operations are involved.

2.11 Summary

By leveraging modules and the powerful compilation process in Erlang, you can build well-structured and efficient applications. Proper use of attributes like -module, -export, and -import enhances code organization. The ability to encapsulate and manage various parts of your application within discrete modules allows for scalability and maintainability.

2.12 Running Erlang Programs

To execute an Erlang program, various methods are available depending on the context and the desired deployment specifics. This section elaborates on running Erlang programs both interactively via the Erlang shell and non-interactively by compiling and executing modules. It is important to understand these mechanisms thoroughly to leverage the full potential of Erlang in both development and production environments.

The Erlang shell is a powerful tool for rapid prototyping and debugging. To start the shell, enter the following command in your terminal:

```
$ erl
```

Once started, you should see the prompt:

```
Eshell V10.7  (abort with ^G)
1>
```

At this point, you can directly input Erlang expressions and execute them. For example, to add two numbers, you can type:

```
1> 2 + 3.
```

The result will be displayed:

```
5
```

For more sophisticated tasks, you will typically write Erlang programs in modules. A module is a file containing a set of functions, typically ending with the '.erl' extension. Below is a sample Erlang module named 'example.erl':

```
-module(example).
-export([start/0]).

start() ->
    io:format("Hello, World!~n").
```

In this module, we define a function start/0 which prints "Hello, World!" to the console. To compile and run this module, perform the following steps:

1. Save the module in a file named 'example.erl'. 2. From the Erlang shell, navigate to the directory containing the file using the cd/1 command:

```
1> cd("path/to/directory").
```

3. To compile the module, use the c/1 function:

```
2> c(example).
```

If the compilation is successful, the following should be displayed:

```
{ok,example}
```

4. To run the compiled module, call the exported start/0 function:

```
3> example:start().
```

The expected output should appear as:

```
Hello, World!
```

When dealing with larger projects, it might be beneficial to use scripts or integrated development environments to manage compilation and execution. For projects containing multiple modules, the make function in the shell can recompile all modified files:

```
4> make:all([load]).
```

This function recompiles all outdated modules and loads them into the running shell environment.

Erlang also supports running programs non-interactively, which is essential for production systems. This is achieved using the 'erl' command with specific options. For example, to run the 'example' module's start/0 function from the command line, use the following command:

```
$ erl -noshell -s example start -s init stop
```

Explanation: - -noshell: Starts Erlang without the shell. - -s example start: Calls the start/0 function from the 'example' module. - -s init stop: Stops the Erlang runtime system after the function executes.

This command will execute the function and then terminate the Erlang runtime system, outputting "Hello, World!" in the terminal without dropping into the interactive shell.

Understanding the process of running Erlang programs efficiently is vital for both development and deployment. Accurate compilation and execution procedures ensure that your programs run as intended, facilitating productive debugging and robust system performance.

2.13 Using the Erlang Documentation

Accessing and utilizing the official Erlang documentation is crucial for effective programming and understanding the language's intricacies. The comprehensive set of resources provided by the Erlang/OTP documentation includes detailed descriptions of libraries, built-in functions, data structures, and system interfaces.

Accessing the Documentation:

The primary source for Erlang documentation is the official Erlang website. It provides an extensive range of documents, including:

- Reference Manuals: Thorough explanations of all the modules and functions available in the standard library.
- User Guides: Detailed guides that provide example-driven explanations of how to use different features and programming constructs.

- API Documentation: Technical details on the APIs provided by Erlang/OTP.
- Man Pages: Manual pages for command-line tools and other utilities provided by Erlang.

Navigating the Documentation:

To effectively navigate the extensive documentation, understanding the structure is essential. The interface often includes:

- Table of Contents (ToC): A hierarchical structure that gives you quick access to different sections and topics.
- Search Functionality: Allows for keyword-based searches, filtering through various documents to find relevant information.
- Index: An alphabetical listing of topics, functions, and modules with links to their respective descriptions.
- Examples: Code samples provided to illustrate the usage of functions and modules.

Using Reference Manuals:

The reference manuals are divided by application and module. Each module document typically includes:

- Overview Section: Brief introduction and purpose of the module.
- Function Specifications: Detailed descriptions of each function, including:
  - Function name
  - Arity (number of arguments)
  - Type specifications (-spec annotations)
  - Return values
  - Side-effects and Exceptions
- Examples: Code snippets demonstrating the functions.

For example, the lists module documentation provides information on various list manipulation functions. To find detailed information on the function lists:map/2, you can refer to the /doc/man/lists.html file or search within the reference manual.

Example: Using lists:map/2

To understand how to use lists:map/2, consider the following code snippet:

```
-module(example).
-export([use_map/0]).

use_map() ->
    Fun = fun(X) -> X * 2 end,
    List = [1, 2, 3, 4],
    lists:map(Fun, List).
```

Upon running this module in the Erlang shell, you obtain:

```
1> c(example).
{ok,example}
2> example:use_map().
[2,4,6,8]
```

This example demonstrates the usage of the lists:map/2 function, which applies the function Fun to each element of List.

Understanding User Guides:

User guides offer more in-depth explanations and practical advice. A typical user guide might cover topics such as:

- Concurrency in Erlang: Explanation of lightweight processes, message passing, and tools like gen_server.
- Building OTP Applications: Steps and best practices for constructing robust applications using the Open Telecom Platform (OTP) framework.
- Error Handling: Techniques for gracefully managing errors and ensuring system stability.

Example: Concurrency in Erlang

Consider a simple example of spawning and communicating between processes:

```
-module(concurrency_example).
-export([start/0, loop/0]).

start() ->
    Pid = spawn(?MODULE, loop, []),
    Pid ! {hello, self()},
    receive
        {ok, Message} -> io:format("Received: ~p~n", [Message])
```

```
    end.

loop() ->
    receive
        {hello, From} ->
            From ! {ok, "Hello, World!"}
    end.
```

Compile and execute the module as follows:

```
1> c(concurrency_example).
{ok,concurrency_example}
2> concurrency_example:start().
Received: "Hello, World!"
ok
```

Utilizing Erlang Man Pages:

Man pages are accessible from the command line using the erl -man command, which provides concise information on different Erlang functionalities directly in the terminal.

For instance, to view the man page for the erl shell, you can use:

```
$ erl -man erl
```

This command opens the manual which details various shell commands, options, and environment settings.

Cross-Referencing Documentation:

Effective use of documentation often requires cross-referencing different types of documents. For instance, while developing a complex application, you might consult:

- Reference Manuals for function specifics.
- User Guides for best practices.
- Man Pages for command-line utilities.
- API Documentation for third-party libraries.

By comprehensively utilizing these resources, you ensure a thorough understanding of Erlang/OTP and enhance your development efficiency and proficiency.

Chapter 3

Basic Language Constructs

This chapter delves into the basic language constructs of Erlang. We will discuss atoms and variables, pattern matching, and guards. The chapter also covers control structures, recursion, and iteration. Additionally, topics such as list comprehensions, tuples, records, and binary data and bit syntax will be explored to lay a solid foundation for understanding and utilizing Erlang effectively.

3.1 Atoms and Variables

Atoms and variables make up the most basic elements in Erlang programming. Understanding their usage and constraints is essential for efficiently writing and comprehending Erlang code.

Atoms are constants whose value is their own name. They start with a lowercase letter or are enclosed in single quotes if they contain special characters or start with an uppercase letter. Atoms provide a way to use symbolic names in Erlang to represent states, messages, or various constant values. Below are examples of valid atoms:

```
ok
error
'Some Atom'
'complex@atom'
```

Variable names in Erlang are immutable and must start with an uppercase letter or an underscore (_). Once a variable is bound to a value, it cannot be changed. Variables in Erlang hold data such as numbers, atoms, tuples, lists, or other complex data structures. Here are a few examples of variable assignments in Erlang:

```
Var1 = 10.
_Name = "Erlang".
```

Because Erlang is a functional language, variable immutability enforces functional programming principles by ensuring values remain constant throughout their scope.

Atoms are a fundamental data type in Erlang, used extensively throughout the language, particularly in pattern matching and message passing. Because Erlang does not support many native data types compared to other languages, atoms often serve as enumerators to represent statuses, operations, commands, and structure tags. For instance:

```
%% Defining atoms
Start = 'start',
Stop = 'stop',
Status = ok.
```

Atoms, being globally unique and immutable, make them efficient for equality checks. The atom's constant nature means that it can be relied upon anywhere in the code without worrying about its value changing.

Atoms that include special characters, spaces, or start with an uppercase letter are enclosed in single quotes. Examples include:

```
'Atom with spaces',
'Another@Atom',
'UPPERCASE'.
```

Variables provide a means to store and manipulate data within the constraints of Erlang's functional paradigm. Since Erlang variables are single-assignment, they can only be bound once within a given context. Any attempt to reassign a variable results in an error. Consider the following example:

```
A = 5,
A = 10. %% This will cause a runtime error
```

Variable names should be descriptive to improve code readability and maintainability. Since the Erlang compiler does not enforce or suggest variable naming conventions, it is essential to follow community-supported guidelines for best practices. For instance:

```
UserName = "Alice",
AccountBalance = 100.50.
```

Variable scope in Erlang is defined by the context where it is created. For example, within a function, once the function call is complete, the variables cease to exist.

One of the key strengths of Erlang is its pattern matching capabilities. Variables play an integral role in this mechanism. When a variable is used in a pattern, it matches the corresponding part of the data structure and gets bound to it. For instance:

```
%% Pattern matching with variables
{Name, Age, Status} = {"Alice", 30, ok}.
```

In this example, Name is bound to "Alice", Age to 30, and Status to ok. Pattern matching is not restricted to tuples but is also applied to lists, records, and other data structures.

If a pattern includes a variable already bound to a value, the match succeeds only if the value in the pattern is the same as the value already bound to the variable:

```
%% Example:
X = 10,
{X, 20} = {10, 20}. %% This matches because X is 10
```

Attempting to match a variable to a different value will cause an error:

```
X = 10,
{X, 30} = {20, 30}. %% This causes an error because X is 10
```

In cases where the matched value is irrelevant, an anonymous variable represented by an underscore (_) can be used. The anonymous variable can match any value, but it doesn't bind to anything. This is useful in functions or patterns where parts of the data structure are not needed:

```
%% Skipping irrelevant data
{_, Result, _} = {ok, 42, undefined}.
```

In this example, only Result will be bound to 42, while the other elements are ignored.

By understanding and utilizing atoms and variables efficiently, Erlang programmers can create clearer and more reliable code. These constructs form the backbone of pattern matching and functional principles that are critical to mastering Erlang programming.

3.2 Pattern Matching

Pattern matching is a fundamental concept in Erlang, providing an intuitive and powerful mechanism for variable binding, data extraction, and control flow. It enables concise expression of conditions and the decomposition of complex data structures. Below, we will explore various facets of pattern matching, elucidating its syntax, usage, and practical applications.

In Erlang, pattern matching can be applied in equations, function clauses, case expressions, receive statements, and more. In its simplest form, a pattern is matched against a term. If the pattern matches the term, variables within the pattern are bound to corresponding parts of the term.

Consider a basic example:

```
X = 10.
```

Here, the pattern X matches the term 10. Consequently, the variable X is bound to the value 10. Pattern matching transcends simple variable assignments and is enabled for complex data structures such as tuples, lists, and maps.

Example with tuples:

```
{Y, Z} = {20, 30}.
```

In this example, the tuple pattern {Y, Z} matches the tuple {20, 30}, and thus Y is bound to 20 and Z is bound to 30. Patterns may include nested structures:

```
{Name, {D, M, Y}} = {"Alice", {14, 11, 2023}}.
```

In the above statement, Name is bound to "Alice", D to 14, M to 11, and Y to 2023.

When working with lists:

```
[H|T] = [1, 2, 3, 4].
```

Here, the list pattern [H|T] decomposes the list [1, 2, 3, 4], binding H to 1 and T to [2, 3, 4].

Pattern matching is pervasive in function clauses. Each clause consists of a pattern that is matched against the function's arguments. The clause whose pattern matches the given arguments is executed:

```
max(X, Y) when X > Y -> X;
max(X, Y) -> Y.
```

This function definition uses pattern matching with guard sequences. When X is greater than Y, the first clause matches, returning X. Otherwise, the second clause matches, returning Y.

Pattern matching also drives control structures such as case expressions:

```
Data = {ok, Result},
case Data of
    {ok, Res} -> io:format("Success: ~p~n", [Res]);
    {error, Message} -> io:format("Error: ~p~n", [Message])
end.
```

In this example, Data is evaluated against the patterns in the case expression. The pattern {ok, Res} matches, and Res is bound to Result, outputting the success message. If Data were {error, Message}, the error message would be printed instead.

The receive construct also benefits from pattern matching. It allows for selective handling of messages, which is critical in concurrent programming:

```
receive
    {msg, Content} -> io:format("Received: ~p~n", [Content]);
    {error, Reason} -> io:format("Error occurred: ~p~n", [Reason])
after 5000 ->
    io:format("Timeout~n")
end.
```

The receive block waits for messages that match any of the specified patterns. If a message {msg, Content} arrives, Content is processed. Otherwise, if {error, Reason} is received, the error is handled. The after clause specifies a timeout, ensuring the system doesn't wait indefinitely.

Pattern matching is not merely an assignment mechanism; it imposes a declarative constraint-checking paradigm whereby the structure and content of data must align with the specified pattern for execution to proceed. Understanding and leveraging pattern matching is pivotal for exploiting Erlang's capabilities in constructing robust, clear, and maintainable code.

3.3 Guards and Guard Sequences

In Erlang, guards and guard sequences play a crucial role in enhancing the expressiveness and precision of function clauses, case statements, and receive expressions. They allow additional conditions to be specified, which must hold true for the corresponding pattern match to succeed. This section examines the syntax and usage of guards and guard sequences in greater detail, providing you with the necessary understanding to employ these constructs effectively in your Erlang programs.

Guards are introduced after the when keyword and consist of a series of boolean expressions. These expressions are evaluated in the context of a pattern match. If the guard evaluates to true, the match succeeds; otherwise, it fails, and the next pattern (if any) is tried. To illustrate guards, consider the following example:

```
factorial(N) when N == 0 ->
    1;
factorial(N) when N > 0 ->
    N * factorial(N - 1).
```

In this example, the function factorial/1 leverages guards to handle two distinct cases. The guard $N == 0$ ensures that the base case is processed correctly when N is zero, while the guard $N > 0$ conditions the recursive call to the factorial function.

Erlang guards support a rich variety of expressions. The following list summarizes the most commonly used guard expressions:

- Comparison operators: ==, =/=, <, >, =<, >=
- Boolean operators: and, or, not
- Arithmetic operators: +, -, *, /
- Type checks: is_integer/1, is_float/1, is_atom/1, is_tuple/1, etc.

Consider the following example that uses type checks and arithmetic operators in guards:

```
abs_value(X) when is_integer(X), X >= 0 ->
    X;
abs_value(X) when is_integer(X), X < 0 ->
    -X.
```

In the abs_value/1 function, guards ensure that the absolute value is computed correctly for any integer input. The guard is_integer(X) checks whether X is an integer, and the subsequent comparisons verify whether the value is non-negative or negative.

Guard sequences allow you to combine multiple guards using semicolons (;), where each guard in the sequence is tried in order. The sequence evaluates to true if at least one guard evaluates to true. This provides a mechanism to specify alternative conditions for the same pattern. For example:

```
is_even_or_divisible(X) when X rem 2 == 0; X rem 3 == 0 ->
    true;
is_even_or_divisible(_) ->
    false.
```

In this function, is_even_or_divisible/1, we use a guard sequence to check if X is either even or divisible by 3. The semicolon between the guards indicates that these are alternative conditions; if either X rem 2 == 0 or X rem 3 == 0 evaluates to true, the function returns true.

When working with guards and guard sequences, it is crucial to be aware of the following important points:

- Guards do not have side effects. They are confined to pure expressions that evaluate without altering the state of the system.
- Only certain BIFs (built-in functions) are allowed in guards, such as length/1, hd/1, tl/1, and type checks. Arbitrary function calls are not permitted.
- Guards should be used to validate constraints that need to be checked before proceeding with a clause execution. They help enforce correctness and improve the robustness of function definitions.

An example of using a guard to enforce a constraint could be observed in the following code:

```
calculate_grade(Score) when is_integer(Score), Score >= 0, Score =< 100 ->
    case Score of
        Score when Score >= 90 -> 'A';
        Score when Score >= 80 -> 'B';
        Score when Score >= 70 -> 'C';
        Score when Score >= 60 -> 'D';
        _ -> 'F'
    end.
```

In calculate_grade/1, guards verify that Score is an integer within the range 0 to 100 before proceeding to the case statement. Each clause within the case statement further refines the criteria using guards to determine the grade based on the score.

Understanding and appropriately utilizing guards and guard sequences enable the creation of more robust, readable, and maintainable Erlang code. They are an integral part of the language's pattern matching mechanism, enhancing the specificity and predictability of function clauses and control structures.

3.4 Control Structures

Erlang provides several control structures to manage the flow of a program. The primary control structures in Erlang include *if*, *case*, and *receive*. This section will explore these constructs in detail, elucidating their syntax and providing practical examples to demonstrate their applications.

The if Expression

The if expression is used to evaluate conditions. It consists of one or more guard sequences, each followed by an expression to execute if the guard sequence evaluates to true. The general syntax of an if expression is as follows:

```
if
    GuardSeq1 -> Expression1;
    GuardSeq2 -> Expression2;
    ...
    GuardSeqN -> ExpressionN
end
```

Each GuardSeq is a condition that evaluates to either true or false. If one of the guard sequences evaluates to true, the corresponding expression is executed. If none of the guard sequences evaluates to true, a if_clause runtime error occurs. To handle such cases, it is common to include a fallback guard sequence that always evaluates to true:

```
if
    Condition1 -> do_something();
    true -> do_default()
end
```

In this example, if none of the conditions are met, the true -> do_default() clause ensures that the if expression still returns a value.

The case Expression

The case expression is one of the most powerful control structures in Erlang, allowing for pattern matching against the value of an expression. The syntax for a case expression is:

```
case Expression of
    Pattern1 [when GuardSeq1] -> Expression1;
    Pattern2 [when GuardSeq2] -> Expression2;
    ...
    PatternN [when GuardSeqN] -> ExpressionN
end
```

Here, the value of Expression is matched against the patterns (Pattern1, Pattern2, ..., PatternN). If a match is found and the guard sequence (if present) evaluates to true, the corresponding expression is executed. If no pattern matches, a case_clause runtime error occurs.

Consider the following example, which demonstrates the use of the case expression:

```
case calculate_value() of
    1 -> io:format("Value is one~n");
    2 -> io:format("Value is two~n");
    _ -> io:format("Value is something else~n")
end
```

In this case, the function calculate_value() returns a value that is matched against the patterns 1, 2, and _. The underscore (_) is a wildcard pattern that matches any value, ensuring that there is always a match, thus preventing a runtime error.

The receive Expression

Erlang's concurrency model relies heavily on the receive expression to handle messages sent between processes. The receive expression waits for a message that matches one of its patterns and then executes the corresponding expression. The syntax for a receive expression is:

```
receive
    Pattern1 [when GuardSeq1] -> Expression1;
    Pattern2 [when GuardSeq2] -> Expression2;
    ...
    PatternN [when GuardSeqN] -> ExpressionN
end
```

When a message is received, it is matched against the patterns (Pattern1, Pattern2, ..., PatternN). If a matching pattern is found, and the corresponding guard sequence (if present) evaluates to true, the associated expression is executed. If no matching message is immediately available, the process waits.

The following example demonstrates a simple use of the receive expression:

```
receive
    {hello, Name} -> io:format("Hello, ~s!~n", [Name]);
    {goodbye, Name} -> io:format("Goodbye, ~s!~n", [Name])
end
```

In this example, the process waits for messages that match either the {hello, Name} pattern or the {goodbye, Name} pattern. Upon receiving a matching message, it prints a greeting or a farewell using the io:format function.

Handling Timeouts in receive Expressions

It is often necessary to handle cases where a message may not be received within a certain timeframe. Erlang's receive expression supports timeouts to address such scenarios. The timeout is specified using the after clause:

```
receive
    Pattern1 [when GuardSeq1] -> Expression1;
    Pattern2 [when GuardSeq2] -> Expression2;
    ...
    PatternN [when GuardSeqN] -> ExpressionN
after Time -> TimeoutExpression
end
```

The Time is given in milliseconds. If no message matching any of the patterns is received within the specified time, the TimeoutExpression is executed. Here is an example:

```
receive
    {hello, Name} -> io:format("Hello, ~s!~n", [Name]);
    {goodbye, Name} -> io:format("Goodbye, ~s!~n", [Name])
after 5000 ->
    io:format("Timeout occurred~n")
end
```

In this example, if no message matching either pattern is received within 5000 milliseconds, the timeout expression prints a timeout message.

Understanding and effectively using control structures in Erlang is crucial for managing the flow of a program, making decisions based on dynamic conditions, and handling concurrency in a reliable manner while ensuring readability and maintainability of the code.

3.5 Recursion and Iteration

Erlang, as a functional programming language, handles iteration differently from imperative languages. In Erlang, recursion is a fundamental concept and the primary mechanism for iteration. Understanding recursion and how to leverage it effectively is crucial for writing idiomatic and efficient Erlang code.

Recursion involves a function calling itself to break down the problem into manageable subproblems. This concept is essential in Erlang due to its immutable state and lack of traditional loop constructs. On the other hand, while Erlang does not have explicit iteration constructs like for loops, list comprehensions provide a powerful and expressive alternative for many iterative operations.

Simple Recursive Functions

A basic example of recursion in Erlang is the factorial function, defined as follows:

```
fac(0) -> 1;
fac(N) when N > 0 -> N * fac(N-1).
```

In this example, fac/1 is a function that computes the factorial of a non-negative integer N. The function consists of two clauses: the base case and the recursive case. The base case fac(0) -> 1; defines that the factorial of 0 is 1. The recursive case fac(N) when N > 0 -> N * fac(N-1). specifies that for any positive integer N, the factorial is N multiplied by the factorial of N-1.

When fac is called with an argument, Erlang evaluates which clause matches. If N is 0, the base case is selected, returning 1. If N is greater than 0, the recursive clause is selected, and fac(N-1) is called. This process continues until N is reduced to 0, at which point the base case is triggered.

Tail Recursion

In some cases, recursive functions can lead to performance issues due to growing call stacks and potential stack overflow errors. Tail recursion, a special form of recursion where the recursive call is the last operation in the function, is often used to mitigate these issues. Tail-recursive functions are optimized by the Erlang runtime system to reuse the current function's stack frame, effectively converting the recursion into iteration.

Consider the following tail-recursive version of the factorial function:

```
fac_tail(N) -> fac_tail(N, 1).

fac_tail(0, Acc) -> Acc;
fac_tail(N, Acc) when N > 0 -> fac_tail(N-1, N * Acc).
```

Here, fac_tail/2 introduces an accumulator parameter Acc to hold the intermediate results. The fac_tail/1 function initializes the recursion with Acc set to 1 and then calls fac_tail/2. In fac_tail/2, the base case fac_tail(0, Acc) -> Acc; returns the value of Acc when N is 0. The recursive case fac_tail(N, Acc) when N > 0 -> fac_tail(N-1, N * Acc). calls itself with N-1 and the updated accumulator N * Acc. This structure ensures that the recursive call is in the tail position, enabling the Erlang runtime to perform tail-call optimization.

Common Recursive Patterns

Recursion is not limited to arithmetic computations. It's also widely used for tasks such as traversing and manipulating lists. A common example is the sum of elements in a list:

```
sum([]) -> 0;
sum([Head | Tail]) -> Head + sum(Tail).
```

In this function, sum/1 recursively traverses the list. The base case sum([]) -> 0; returns 0 when the list is empty. The recursive case sum([Head | Tail]) -> Head + sum(Tail). deconstructs the list into its head and tail, adds the head to the result of the sum of the tail, and continues this pattern until the list is empty.

To convert this into a tail-recursive function, we can introduce an accumulator parameter:

```
sum_tail(List) -> sum_tail(List, 0).

sum_tail([], Acc) -> Acc;
sum_tail([Head | Tail], Acc) -> sum_tail(Tail, Acc + Head).
```

sum_tail/2 uses Acc to accumulate the sum of the elements. The base case sum_tail([], Acc) -> Acc; returns the accumulated sum when the list is empty. The recursive case sum_tail([Head | Tail], Acc) -> sum_tail(Tail, Acc + Head). updates the accumulator by adding the head of the list and recurses with the tail.

List Comprehensions

Erlang provides list comprehensions as an alternative to explicit recursion for many common list operations. List comprehensions are more concise and often more readable. The sum of a list using list comprehensions can be expressed as follows:

```
sum(List) -> lists:sum([X || X <- List]).
```

Here, the list comprehension [X || X <- List] generates a new list containing the elements of List. The lists:sum/1 function from the lists module then computes the sum of the generated list. This approach abstracts away the explicit recursion, providing a more declarative and expressive syntax.

Another example of using list comprehensions is filtering elements. Consider a function that selects even numbers from a list:

```
filter_even(List) -> [X || X <- List, X rem 2 == 0].
```

The list comprehension generates a new list including only elements X from List where X rem 2 == 0, i.e., where X is even. This concise representation can enhance readability and reduce the likelihood of errors compared to explicit recursive implementations.

In Erlang, recursion is not only a powerful tool for defining iterative processes but also an essential technique for working with immutable data structures. Tail recursion optimizes performance and prevents stack overflow risks. List comprehensions offer a syntactically elegant and expressive means to manipulate lists, providing alternatives to manual recursion in many scenarios. Combining these constructs enables the writing of robust, efficient, and concise Erlang code.

3.6 List Comprehensions

List comprehensions in Erlang offer a powerful and expressive way to construct lists. They are syntactic constructs that enable the creation of new lists by specifying a pattern and a set of rules. The basic syntax of a list comprehension can be represented as follows:

```
[Expression || Pattern <- List, Condition1, Condition2, ...]
```

Here, Expression represents the operation to be performed on each element of the List that matches the Pattern. The optional Condition1, Condition2, ... are Boolean expressions that filter the elements.

- Generating Simple Lists

Consider an example where we want to generate a list containing the squares of integers from 1 to 10:

```
Squares = [X * X || X <- lists:seq(1, 10)].
```

In this case, lists:seq(1, 10) generates a list of integers from 1 to 10. Each integer X in this list is then squared, resulting in the Squares list.

```
[1, 4, 9, 16, 25, 36, 49, 64, 81, 100]
```

- Adding Conditions

Conditions can be added to a list comprehension to filter out elements that do not meet certain criteria. For instance, if we want to generate a list of even squares from 1 to 10:

```
EvenSquares = [X * X || X <- lists:seq(1, 10), X rem 2 == 0].
```

Here, X rem 2 == 0 ensures that only even numbers from 1 to 10 are considered for squaring.

```
[4, 16, 36, 64, 100]
```

- Nested Generators

List comprehensions also support multiple generators, which can be used to iterate over multiple lists. Suppose we want to create pairs of elements from two different lists:

```
Pairs = [{X, Y} || X <- [1, 2], Y <- [a, b]].
```

This comprehension pairs each element of the first list with each element of the second list.

```
[{1,a},{1,b},{2,a},{2,b}]
```

- Combining Generators and Conditions

We can combine multiple generators and conditions for more complex list comprehensions. For example, generating pairs of elements where the sum of the pair is greater than 4:

```
FilteredPairs = [{X, Y} || X <- [1, 2, 3, 4], Y <- [1, 2, 3, 4], X + Y > 4].
```

In this example, $X + Y > 4$ filters out pairs whose sums do not meet the condition.

[{1,4},{2,3},{2,4},{3,2},{3,3},{3,4},{4,1},{4,2},{4,3},{4,4}]

- Practical Example: Pythagorean Triples

A well-known problem in list comprehensions is the generation of Pythagorean triples, which are sets of three integers (a, b, c) such that $a\hat{}2 + b\hat{}2 = c\hat{}2$. To generate such triples within a certain range, we can use the following list comprehension:

```
PythagoreanTriples = [{A, B, C} ||
                      A <- lists:seq(1, 20),
                      B <- lists:seq(A, 20),
                      C <- lists:seq(B, 20),
                      A * A + B * B == C * C].
```

The generators ensure that A, B, C are each taken from the range 1 to 20, and the condition $A * A + B * B == C * C$ ensures that only valid triples are included.

[{3,4,5},{5,12,13},{6,8,10},{8,15,17},{9,12,15},{12,16,20}]

- Efficiency Considerations

While list comprehensions are concise and expressive, they may not always be the most efficient choice for all problems. For large lists or performance-critical applications, it is essential to consider the computational complexity and potential memory usage of the generated lists. Factors such as the number of elements and the nature of the conditions can significantly impact performance.

List comprehensions provide a versatile tool for working with lists in Erlang, enabling the concise expression of complex list operations.

3.7 Tuples and Records

Tuples and records are two fundamental data structures in Erlang that are essential for organizing and storing related data. While both serve the purpose of grouping elements, they are used in different scenarios and have distinct properties. Understanding these constructs is crucial for writing efficient and maintainable Erlang code.

Tuples are fixed-size collections used to group together a fixed number of elements. Each element in a tuple can be of any data type, and they are enclosed in curly braces { }. The elements within a tuple are accessed by their position.

```
% Defining a tuple
Person = {"John", 30, "Engineer"}.

% Accessing elements in a tuple
Name = element(1, Person). % Returns "John"
Age = element(2, Person). % Returns 30
Occupation = element(3, Person). % Returns "Engineer"
```

Tuples are particularly useful when the number of elements and their order are known and fixed. While they offer a straightforward way to group data, modifying elements within a tuple requires creating a new tuple, as tuples are immutable.

```
% Updating an element in a tuple
NewPerson = setelement(2, Person, 31). % Changes age to 31
```

Records, on the other hand, are syntactic sugar on top of tuples that provide a convenient way to manage structured data with named fields. Records improve code readability and maintainability by allowing fields to be accessed by name rather than position. To define a record, you must declare its structure using the -record directive.

```
% Defining a record
-record(person, {name, age, occupation}).

% Creating a record instance
John = #person{name="John", age=30, occupation="Engineer"}.
```

One of the main advantages of records is the ability to access and update fields by name, making the code easier to understand and maintain.

```
% Accessing fields in a record
Name = John#person.name. % Returns "John"
Age = John#person.age. % Returns 30

% Updating fields in a record
OlderJohn = John#person{age=31}.
```

When working with records, it is important to include the record definition file in the modules where the record is used. This can be done using the -include or -include_lib directive.

```
% Including a record definition file
-include("person.hrl").
```

Records can also be utilized in pattern matching to destructure data and extract values conveniently.

```
% Pattern matching with records
handle_person(#person{name=Name, age=Age} = Person) ->
    io:format("Name: ~s, Age: ~p~n", [Name, Age]),
    Person.
```

In comparison to tuples, records provide a higher level of abstraction and are recommended for more complex data structures where field names enhance code clarity.

It is worth noting that records in Erlang are not a built-in data type but are compiled down to tuples. This means that all the benefits of using records come with no additional runtime overhead, as they are essentially tuples with named fields. However, this also means that when records are printed or serialized, they appear as tuples.

```
#person{name="John", age=30, occupation="Engineer"}.
% When printed, this appears as:
{person, "John", 30, "Engineer"}.
```

Understanding when to use tuples and when to use records is important for efficient data management in Erlang applications. Tuples are ideal for smaller, fixed-size collections where positional access suffices, while records are preferred for larger, more complex data structures where named fields and improved readability are beneficial.

3.8 Binary Data and Bit Syntax

Binary data and bit syntax in Erlang provide powerful mechanisms for pattern matching directly on sequences of bytes, enabling efficient and flexible processing of binary formats such as network protocols and file formats. Erlang's bit syntax allows for precise manipulation of binary data and often simplifies the handling of complex binaries that need to be processed or constructed bit by bit.

Introduction to Binary Data Type:

The binary data type is represented by the binary() type. It is enclosed within double angle brackets, « and ». Each element in the binary is termed a "bitstring," which may consist of multiple binary segments.

```
Data = <<"Hello, World!">>,
```

The Data variable holds a binary value representing the string "Hello, World!"

Constructing Binaries:

In Erlang, you can construct binary data by specifying values within double angle brackets. Each value can be an integer, a float, or another binary, optionally specifying the number of bits it occupies.

```
Binary1 = <<255>>,
Binary2 = <<255:16>>,
Binary3 = <<3.14/float>>,
Binary4 = <<1,2,3,4>>,
Binary5 = <<"Erlang">>,
Binary6 = <<Bin1/binary, Bin2/binary>>
```

- Binary1 is an 8-bit binary representing the number 255.
- Binary2 is a 16-bit binary where 255 are expressed in two bytes: 0x00FF.
- Binary3 is a binary representing the floating point number 3.14.
- Binary4 is a 4-byte binary concatenating four integers.
- Binary5 is a binary encoding the string "Erlang".
- Binary6 concatenates two existing binaries Bin1 and Bin2.

Pattern Matching on Binaries:

Erlang provides the ability to pattern match directly on binary data. The structure of the binary can be matched in a specific format by utilizing the bit syntax.

```
<<A:8, B:16, C:32>> = <<1,2,3,4,5,6,7>>
```

Here, A will be 1, a single 8-bit integer, B will interpret the next 16 bits as an integer (512), and C will take the next 32 bits.

Specifying Bit Sizes and Types:

The general syntax for a segment in Erlang's bit syntax includes the size of the segment and the type. The complete specification format is Value:Size/TypeSpecifier.

- Value:Size specifies the size in bits.
- TypeSpecifier determines the type, such as integer, float, binary, etc.

```
Bin = <<1:8/integer, 2:24/little, 3:16/big-unsigned, 4:32/float>>
```

Composing and Decomposing Binaries:

Erlang's bit syntax is especially useful in decomposing complex binary formats.

```
Packet = <<Version:8, Length:16, Payload/binary>>,
<<Version:4, Header:4, Body/binary>> = Packet
```

```
Version: 0x1
Header: 0x0
Body: binary(...)
```

Binary Comprehensions:

Similar to list comprehensions, Erlang offers binary comprehensions for generating and transforming binaries.

```
Bin = << <<(X * 2):8>> || X <- [1,2,3,4] >>
```

```
<<2,4,6,8>>
```

Advanced Binary Construction:

Multiple fields with mixed types can be combined into a single binary. This combines integers, floats, or binaries of designated sizes ensuring efficient and compact binary formation.

```
Bin = <<X1:16/integer, X2:32/signed-big, Y1:64/float>>
```

Proper use of bit syntax enhances readability, reduces computational overhead, and optimizes memory usage when handling binary data. When working with network protocols, file parsing, or any domain requiring manipulation at a bit level, Erlang's binary data and bit syntax are invaluable tools.

Chapter 4

Working with Data Structures

This chapter focuses on Erlang's data structures, covering lists, tuples, maps, and records. It explains their creation, manipulation, and use cases. Further, it explores working with sets and handling binary data, emphasizing efficiency considerations. The goal is to provide comprehensive knowledge to effectively leverage these data structures in Erlang programming.

4.1 Introduction to Data Structures in Erlang

Erlang, a concurrent functional programming language, provides a variety of data structures essential for effective programming. These data structures include lists, tuples, maps, and records, each with unique characteristics and use cases. An understanding of these fundamental components is crucial for mastering Erlang and leveraging its capabilities for building robust and efficient applications.

Lists in Erlang are linked lists, which makes their operations generally efficient for activities such as adding or removing elements at the head of the list. Lists can be dynamically resized, allowing them to hold an arbitrary number of elements. This makes them suitable for representing sequences of data where frequent insertions and deletions are necessary.

```
List1 = [1, 2, 3, 4].
List2 = ["apple", "banana", "cherry"].
```

```
# Output:
[1,2,3,4]
["apple","banana","cherry"]
```

Tuples, on the other hand, are fixed-size collections of elements. Unlike lists, they offer constant-time access to elements, making them suitable when the number of elements is known, and random access is required. Tuples are frequently used to store fixed related data, such as coordinates, or to return multiple values from a function.

```
Tuple1 = {ok, "Success"}.
Tuple2 = {4, 5, 6}.
```

```
# Output:
{ok,"Success"}
{4,5,6}
```

Maps in Erlang provide key-value storage, allowing efficient lookups, insertions, and deletions. Maps are particularly useful for representing associative arrays and dictionaries. Unlike lists and tuples, maps do not maintain the order of elements.

```
Map1 = #{name => "John", age => 25}.
Map2 = #{language => "Erlang", level => "advanced"}.
```

```
# Output:
#{name => "John", age => 25}
#{language => "Erlang", level => "advanced"}
```

Records are syntactic sugar on top of tuples that provide structured data storage with named fields. Records are defined using the record keyword and are particularly useful for handling structured data where referencing fields by name improves readability and maintainability.

```
-record(person, {name, age}).
Person = #person{name = "Alice", age = 30}.
```

```
# Output:
Person = #person{name = "Alice", age = 30}
```

The semantics of data structure manipulation involve functions and operations tailored to each type's properties. For instance, lists have functions such as lists:map/2 for mapping a function over a list, lists:filter/2 for filtering elements, and ++ for list concatenation.

```
List1 = [1, 2, 3],
List2 = [4, 5, 6],
List3 = List1 ++ List2.
Filtered = lists:filter(fun(X) -> X rem 2 == 0 end, List3).
```

```
# Output:
[1,2,3,4,5,6]
[2,4,6]
```

Tuples utilize built-in operators for accessing elements such as element/2 and setelement/3 to modify values at specific positions.

```
Tuple = {1, 2, 3},
Element = element(2, Tuple),
NewTuple = setelement(2, Tuple, 99).
```

```
# Output:
2
{1, 99, 3}
```

Maps have a robust suite of functions such as maps:get/2 for retrieving values, maps:put/3 for inserting key-value pairs, and maps:remove/2 for deleting entries.

```
Map = #{a => 1, b => 2},
Value = maps:get(a, Map),
NewMap = maps:put(c, 3, Map),
FinalMap = maps:remove(b, NewMap).
```

```
# Output:
1
#{a => 1, b => 2, c => 3}
#{a => 1, c => 3}
```

Records simplify working with structured data by allowing access through named fields. They support operations to get and set values efficiently using pattern matching and record syntax.

```
-record(user, {id, name, age}).
User = #user{id = 1, name = "Alice", age = 30},
Name = User#user.name,
UpdatedUser = User#user{age = 31}.
```

```
# Output:
"Alice"
#user{id = 1, name = "Alice", age = 31}
```

Each data structure in Erlang serves specific purposes, driven by their inherent properties, operational efficiencies, and syntactic conveniences. Proficiency in using these structures involves not only understanding their definitions and operations but also insight into optimal scenarios for their application. As we progressively delve into lists, tuples, maps, and records in subsequent sections, a comprehensive grasp of their foundational concepts will be indispensable.

4.2 Lists: Creation and Manipulation

In Erlang, lists are one of the fundamental data structures, offering both flexibility and simplicity for storing and manipulating collections of elements. Lists can contain any kind of values, including other lists, enabling the creation of complex, nested structures. This section delves into the creation, operations, and manipulations of lists.

Creating Lists

Lists in Erlang are created using square brackets. Elements of the list are separated by commas. For example:

```
% An empty list
EmptyList = [].

% A list of integers
IntegerList = [1, 2, 3, 4, 5].

% A list containing mixed types
MixedList = [1, "two", 3.0, {four, 4}, [5]].
```

Basic Operations on Lists

Several basic operations can be performed on lists, including concatenation, list construction using the cons operator, and list pattern matching.

List Concatenation: Lists can be concatenated using the ++ operator.

```
List1 = [1, 2],
List2 = [3, 4],
ConcatenatedList = List1 ++ List2.
```

The value of ConcatenatedList will be [1, 2, 3, 4].

The Cons Operator: The cons operator (|) is used to construct lists. It takes an element and a list, placing the element at the head of the list.

```
% Using the cons operator
Head = 1,
Tail = [2, 3, 4],
List = [Head | Tail].
```

The value of List will be [1, 2, 3, 4].

List Pattern Matching: Erlang allows powerful pattern matching capabilities, especially useful with lists. This feature is often used in function heads and case expressions.

```
% Pattern matching on a list
[Head | Tail] = [1, 2, 3, 4].
```

In this case, Head will be bound to 1, and Tail will be bound to [2, 3, 4].

Common List Functions

Erlang's standard library provides several functions for manipulating lists, located in the lists module. These functions are instrumental for various operations.

length/1: The length/1 function returns the number of elements in a list.

```
List = [1, 2, 3, 4, 5],
ListLength = length(List).
```

The value of ListLength will be 5.

reverse/1: The reverse/1 function returns a new list with the elements in reverse order.

```
List = [1, 2, 3, 4, 5],
ReversedList = lists:reverse(List).
```

The value of ReversedList will be [5, 4, 3, 2, 1].

map/2: The map/2 function applies a given function to each element of a list and returns a new list with the results.

```
% Define a simple increment function
Increment = fun(X) -> X + 1 end,
List = [1, 2, 3, 4, 5],
MappedList = lists:map(Increment, List).
```

The value of MappedList will be [2, 3, 4, 5, 6].

filter/2: The filter/2 function returns a new list containing only the elements that satisfy a specified condition.

```
% Define a predicate to filter even numbers
IsEven = fun(X) -> X rem 2 == 0 end,
List = [1, 2, 3, 4, 5],
FilteredList = lists:filter(IsEven, List).
```

The value of FilteredList will be [2, 4].

foldl/3 and foldr/3: These functions are used to accumulate values by applying a function to the elements of a list, either from the left (foldl) or right (foldr).

```
% Sum a list of integers using foldl
Sum = fun(X, Acc) -> X + Acc end,
List = [1, 2, 3, 4, 5],
Total = lists:foldl(Sum, 0, List).
```

The value of Total will be 15.

List Comprehensions

List comprehensions provide a concise way to create lists based on existing lists. The syntax includes an expression followed by a generator, with optional filters. The generator specifies how to form elements of the new list from elements of the existing list.

```
% Create a list of squares
Squares = [X*X || X <- [1, 2, 3, 4, 5]].

% Create a list of even numbers
Evens = [X || X <- [1, 2, 3, 4, 5], X rem 2 == 0].
```

The value of Squares will be [1, 4, 9, 16, 25] and the value of Evens will be [2, 4].

Complex List Operations

In addition to basic and common operations, complex manipulations are often necessary. These may involve nested list comprehensions, multiple filters, or combining lists in non-trivial ways.

```
% Flatten a list of lists
NestedList = [[1, 2], [3, 4], [5]],
FlattenedList = lists:append(NestedList).

% Cartesian product of two lists
List1 = [1, 2],
List2 = [a, b],
CartesianProduct = [{X, Y} || X <- List1, Y <- List2].
```

The value of FlattenedList will be [1, 2, 3, 4, 5] and the value of CartesianProduct will be [1, a, 1, b, 2, a, 2, b].

Understanding and efficiently working with lists are crucial skills. As demonstrated, Erlang's list handling capabilities provide powerful tools to create and manipulate lists with a high degree of expressiveness and functionality.

4.3 Tuples: Creation and Use Cases

Tuples are a fundamental data structure in Erlang, providing a way to group fixed numbers of elements into a single compound data type. They are an ordered collection of elements, where each element can be of any data type, including other tuples. Unlike lists, tuples are typically used for fixed-size collections of related elements, often for representing records or configurations. To leverage the full utility of tuples, we will explore their creation, manipulation, and typical use cases in this section.

Creating a tuple in Erlang is straightforward. A tuple is denoted by curly braces {} enclosing its elements, separated by commas. For example, a tuple containing an integer, an atom, and a string can be written as:

```
Module = {1, example, "This is a tuple"}.
```

This tuple consists of three elements: the integer 1, the atom example, and the string "This is a tuple". To access an element within a tuple, we use the built-in function element/2. The first argument of element/2 is the position (1-based index) of the element within the tuple, and the second argument is the tuple itself. For instance, to retrieve the second element of the previously created tuple:

```
SecondElement = element(2, Module).
```

The variable SecondElement will now hold the value example. It is important to note that element positions in tuples start at 1, not 0. To replace an element at a specific position within a tuple, we use the setelement/3 function. Its first argument is the position to be replaced, the second argument is the tuple, and the third argument is the new value. For example, to replace the first element of Module with the atom updated:

```
UpdatedModule = setelement(1, Module, updated).
```

Tuples are immutable data structures in Erlang, meaning that any modification results in the creation of a new tuple, leaving the original one unchanged. This property aligns with Erlang's functional programming paradigm and its emphasis on immutable state. Because tuples are fixed in size, they are not suitable for operations that frequently change the number of elements, such as appending or removing elements, for which lists are more appropriate.

A typical use case for tuples is to represent coordinates in a 2D plane. For instance, a point can be defined by a tuple containing two integers, representing the x and y coordinates:

```
Point = {10, 20}.
```

To make computations with points, we can define functions that operate on these tuples. Suppose we want to calculate the distance between two points. We can achieve this by defining a function as follows:

```
distance({X1, Y1}, {X2, Y2}) ->
    Math:sqrt((X2 - X1) * (X2 - X1) + (Y2 - Y1) * (Y2 - Y1)).
```

By calling this function with two point tuples, we can obtain the Euclidean distance between them:

```
D = distance({10, 20}, {13, 24}).
```

D will contain the result of the distance calculation.

Tuples are also frequently used in pattern matching, a powerful feature in Erlang. For example, when writing functions, we can match on the structure of tuples directly in function heads or case expressions. Consider a function that determines the type of a geometric shape based on a tuple:

```
shape({rectangle, _, _}) -> "This is a rectangle";
shape({circle, _}) -> "This is a circle";
shape({triangle, _, _, _}) -> "This is a triangle";
shape(_) -> "Unknown shape".
```

When called with a specific tuple, the respective clause will match and execute:

```
ShapeType = shape({circle, 10}).
```

```
"This is a circle"
```

The above function shape/1 demonstrates how tuples facilitate concise and readable code through pattern matching. This ability to destructure tuples into their constituent parts allows for dynamic and flexible function definitions.

Moreover, tuples are adept at representing configurations and key-value pairs in a compact manner, often seen in Erlang's standard libraries and OTP framework. For example, consider a tuple representing a user configuration:

```
UserConfig = {username, "alice", permissions, [read, write]}.
```

Here, username and permissions are key-value pairs within the tuple, denoting the user's name and a list of their permissions. This illustrates how tuples can efficiently encode structured data in a fixed format.

In scenarios requiring consistent and high-speed access to elements, tuples are often preferred due to their constant-time access properties. Unlike lists, where access time depends on the element's position, tuple access performs in $O(1)$ time complexity, making it an optimal choice for small, fixed-size collections.

Tuples' immutability, ability to store heterogeneous elements, and constant-time access make them invaluable in many Erlang applications, from system configurations to data representation in algorithms. Understanding the intricacies of tuple manipulation and their optimal use cases is crucial for efficient and effective Erlang programming.

4.4 Maps: Key-Value Storage

Maps are fundamental data structures in Erlang, offering an efficient way to store and retrieve key-value pairs. A map is an unordered collection, where each key is unique and associated with a specific value. Key-value storage is particularly useful in scenarios where quick lookup of data is required based on an associated key. This section delves into the creation, manipulation, and typical use cases of maps in Erlang to provide a comprehensive understanding of their application.

Creating Maps

Maps in Erlang can be created using the #{} syntax. A map can be defined with initial key-value pairs by listing them inside the curly braces.

```
% Creating a new map with initial key-value pairs
Map1 = #{ name => "Alice", age => 30, city => "New York" }.
```

In this example, Map1 is a map containing three key-value pairs. The keys are name, age, and city, each associated with their respective values.

Accessing Values in Maps

Values in a map can be accessed using the maps:get/2 function or the map key operator =>. The maps:get/2 function requires the key and the map as arguments.

```
% Accessing the value associated with the key 'name'
Name = maps:get(name, Map1). % Returns "Alice"
```

Alternatively, the map key operator can be used for more concise code.

```
% Using the map key operator to access the value
Name = Map1#{ name }. % Returns "Alice"
```

When using the key operator, if the key does not exist in the map, an error will be thrown. To handle such cases gracefully, maps:find/2 can be utilized, which returns either {ok, Value} or error.

```
% Safely finding a key in the map
case maps:find(city, Map1) of
    {ok, City} -> io:format("City: ~s~n", [City]);
    error -> io:format("City not found~n")
end.
```

Updating Maps

Maps in Erlang are immutable, meaning an update operation actually creates a new map with the desired modifications while leaving the original map untouched. The maps:put/3 function or #{} syntax can be used to update maps. The maps:put/3 function takes three arguments: the key to update, the new value, and the original map.

```
% Updating the value associated with an existing key
Map2 = maps:put(age, 31, Map1). % Creates a new map with updated age
```

Alternatively, the #{} syntax provides a succinct way to achieve the same result.

```
% Using syntax to update the map
Map2 = Map1#{ age := 31 }.
```

Both methods create a new map Map2 with the age key updated to 31.

Adding and Removing Keys

The process of adding new key-value pairs and removing existing keys follows the principles of immutability. To add a new key-value pair, we can use the maps:put/3 function:

```
% Adding a new key-value pair to the map
Map3 = maps:put(country, "USA", Map2).
```

This results in a new map Map3 containing the additional key country with the value "USA".

Removing a key-value pair involves using the maps:remove/2 function, which takes the key to be removed and the target map.

```
% Removing the key 'city' from the map
Map4 = maps:remove(city, Map3).
```

Merging Maps

Merging two maps can be accomplished using the maps:merge/3 function. The third argument is a function that resolves conflicts when a key exists in both maps. This function is applied to the conflicting key's values to produce the resulting value.

```
% Merging two maps with conflict resolution
Map5 = #{ rank => 5, score => 80 }.
Map6 = #{ score => 90, level => 2 }.

% Function to resolve conflicts by choosing the highest value
ConflictResolver = fun(_Key, Val1, Val2) -> max(Val1, Val2) end.

% Merge maps with conflict resolution
MergedMap = maps:merge(ConflictResolver, Map5, Map6).
```

This produces a MergedMap where conflicting keys are resolved using the ConflictResolver function.

```
MergedMap: #{level => 2, rank => 5, score => 90}
```

Common Operations and Functions

- maps:size/1 - Returns the number of key-value pairs in the map.
- maps:keys/1 - Returns a list of all keys in the map.
- maps:values/1 - Returns a list of all values in the map.
- maps:is_key/2 - Checks if a given key exists in the map.

Example usage:

```
% Getting the size of the map
Size = maps:size(MergedMap).

% Retrieving all keys from the map
Keys = maps:keys(MergedMap).

% Retrieving all values from the map
Values = maps:values(MergedMap).

% Checking if a key exists
Exists = maps:is_key(rank, MergedMap).
```

These operations enable effective management and querying of maps, making them a versatile tool in Erlang programming. Maps facilitate efficient data handling, contributing to the language's robust capabilities in building concurrent and distributed systems.

4.5 Records: Structured Data Storage

Records in Erlang provide a structured and efficient way to store related data elements together. They are similar to structs in C or objects in more object-oriented languages. Records are defined using the -record directive and are often used to manage state within a process or to encapsulate data logically.

A record is essentially a predefined tuple where each element is named and can be accessed using its name rather than its position in the tuple. This abstraction simplifies code readability and maintenance by providing meaningful names for elements.

The syntax for defining a record is as follows:

```
-record(record_name, {field1, field2, ..., fieldN}).
```

For example, to define a record representing a person with name, age, and gender, the following definition would be used:

```
-record(person, {name, age, gender}).
```

To create an instance of a record, you use the following syntax:

```
Person = #person{name="Alice", age=30, gender=female}.
```

To access individual fields in a record, use the record field notation #record_name.field:

```
Name = Person#person.name.
```

To update a field in a record, use the following pattern:

```
UpdatedPerson = Person#person{name="Bob"}.
```

Let's delve into more details about records by considering common operations and best practices.

Pattern Matching with Records

One of the notable features of Erlang is its powerful pattern matching capabilities, which extend to records. You can pattern match against records in function heads, case expressions, and receive statements.

Consider the following function that takes a person record and returns a greeting message:

```
greet(#person{name=Name}) ->
    "Hello " ++ Name ++ "!".
```

This function extracts the name field from the person record and constructs a greeting message.

CASE expressions can also utilize pattern matching with records effectively:

```
determine_age_group(Person) ->
    case Person of
        #person{age=A} when A < 18 -> "Child";
        #person{age=A} when A < 65 -> "Adult";
        _ -> "Senior"
    end.
```

Default Values

You can specify default values for record fields when defining the record. If a field is not provided explicitly during record instantiation, it will take its default value.

```
-record(person, {name, age = 0, gender = unknown}).
```

Creating a person record without specifying all fields will use the default values:

```
Person = #person{name="Alice"}.
% Person = #person{name="Alice", age=0, gender=unknown}
```

Records and Modules

Records are often defined in modules where they are used. To avoid redefinitions and ensure consistency, you can define records in header files and include them using the -include directive.

Create a header file person.hrl:

```
%% person.hrl
-record(person, {name, age = 0, gender = unknown}).
```

Include the header file in your module:

```
%% my_module.erl
-module(my_module).
-include("person.hrl").
```

```
create_person(Name) ->
    #person{name=Name}.
```

Record Information and Meta-Programming

Erlang provides facilities for obtaining metadata about records. This metadata can be useful for code introspection and generation.

```
-record(person, {name, age, gender}).

%% Get record information
-record_info(fields, person). % Returns [name, age, gender]
-record_info(size, person). % Returns 4 (number of elements in the tuple)
```

These functions return various types of metadata. For example, -record_info(fields, RecordName) returns a list of the names of the fields in the record, and -record_info(size, RecordName) returns the number of elements in the underlying tuple.

Efficiency Considerations

Records in Erlang are implemented as tuples, and thus inherit the performance characteristics of tuples. Accessing a field in a record using #record_name.field is efficient and involves constant-time complexity. However, updating a record requires copying the original tuple and modifying the required fields, which has a cost proportional to the size of the tuple.

Records should be preferred over tuples when the elements have meaningful names or when the record structure is intended to evolve. By using records, you gain the advantage of code readability and maintenance, especially in larger projects.

Records offer a structured and efficient method for managing related data elements in Erlang. They encapsulate data logically within a predefined structure, enhancing code readability and maintainability. A solid understanding of records is essential for effective Erlang programming, enabling the management of complex data structures with relative ease.

4.6 Working with Sets

Erlang provides a robust and efficient mechanism to work with sets, encapsulated within the sets and gb_sets modules. Both modules serve the purpose of representing a collection of unique elements but differ in their underlying implementations and performance characteristics.

sets module relies on unordered lists, which is suitable for small sets and infrequent operations. On the other hand, **gb_sets** module employs balanced binary trees (General Balanced, GB) providing better performance for larger sets and more frequent operations.

A set is a collection of unique elements where each element appears only once. We will explore key functionalities such as creation, insertion, deletion, and membership testing, pertinent to both sets and gb_sets modules.

Creating Sets

To initialize a new empty set using either the sets or gb_sets module, you can use the following commands:

```
% Using sets module
EmptySet = sets:new().

% Using gb_sets module
EmptyGBSet = gb_sets:new().
```

Both commands create an empty set, but the underlying structure and efficiency differ. sets:new() initializes an unordered list, whereas gb_sets:new() initializes a balanced binary tree.

Inserting Elements

To add elements to a set, the add_element/2 function is used. Given an element and a set, this function inserts the element into the set.

```
% Using sets module
Set1 = sets:new().
Set2 = sets:add_element(1, Set1).
Set3 = sets:add_element(2, Set2).

% Using gb_sets module
GBSet1 = gb_sets:new().
GBSet2 = gb_sets:insert(1, GBSet1).
GBSet3 = gb_sets:insert(2, GBSet2).
```

In both modules, if the element already exists in the set, the structure remains unchanged.

Deleting Elements

Removing an element from a set is achieved using del_element/2 in the sets module or delete/2 in the gb_sets module.

```
% Using sets module
Set4 = sets:del_element(1, Set3).

% Using gb_sets module
GBSet4 = gb_sets:delete(1, GBSet3).
```

After executing these commands, the specified element, if present, will be removed from the set.

Checking Membership

Membership testing checks if a particular element exists within a set using is_element/2:

```
% Using sets module
IsMember = sets:is_element(2, Set3).

% Using gb_sets module
IsMemberGB = gb_sets:is_element(2, GBSet3).
```

In both cases, the function returns true if the element exists within the set and false otherwise.

Set Operations

Erlang supports various operations between sets such as union, intersection, and difference. These operations can be performed using the sets or gb_sets modules.

Union: Combines all unique elements from two sets.

```
% Using sets module
UnionSet = sets:union(Set2, Set3).

% Using gb_sets module
UnionGBSet = gb_sets:union(GBSet2, GBSet3).
```

Intersection: Extracts elements common to both sets.

```
% Using sets module
IntersectionSet = sets:intersection(Set2, Set3).

% Using gb_sets module
IntersectionGBSet = gb_sets:intersection(GBSet2, GBSet3).
```

Difference: Finds elements that are present in the first set but not in the second.

```
% Using sets module
DifferenceSet = sets:subtract(Set3, Set2).

% Using gb_sets module
DifferenceGBSet = gb_sets:subtract(GBSet3, GBSet2).
```

Efficiency Considerations

While both sets and gb_sets aim to provide set functionalities, their performance is influenced by their underlying data structures. The sets module, implemented as unordered lists, generally provides $O(N)$ performance for most operations, where N is the number of elements in the set. This linear time complexity might suffice for small datasets or infrequent operations.

Conversely, the gb_sets module uses balanced binary trees, offering better performance characteristics with $O(\log N)$ complexity for most operations. This logarithmic time complexity makes gb_sets more suitable for larger sets or situations where operations are frequent and performance is critical.

Choosing between these modules depends on the specific use case, balancing between ease of implementation and the need for performance optimization.

4.7 Binary Data Handling

Binary data handling in Erlang is crucial, especially for applications involving communication protocols, file processing, and data serialization or deserialization. Erlang provides powerful constructs for creating, manipulating, and matching binary data. This section delves into binary comprehensions, pattern matching, and efficiency considerations associated with handling binary data.

Binary data in Erlang is represented using the «» syntax, where data elements can be of varying sizes and types. Each element within a binary can be a specific number of bits, rather than just whole bytes. This flexibility allows fine-grained control over data representation and manipulation.

```
% Example of creating a binary
```

```
Binary = <<1, 2, 3, 4>>.
```

The above example creates a binary containing the bytes 1, 2, 3, and 4. By default, each number corresponds to an 8-bit segment (one byte). To specify bit size explicitly, we use the $/Size$ syntax.

```
% Example with explicit bit size
Binary = <<1:8, 2:8, 3:8, 4:8>>.
```

In this example, each number is explicitly defined as 8 bits.

Pattern Matching on Binaries

Pattern matching on binaries allows deconstruction of binary data into components for further processing. This is particularly useful for decoding network packets or parsing file contents.

```
% Pattern matching on a binary
<<A:8, B:8, Rest/binary>> = <<1, 2, 3, 4, 5, 6>>.
```

Here, A and B are matched to the first two bytes of the binary, and $Rest$ to the remaining binary data.

```
A = 1,
B = 2,
Rest = <<3, 4, 5, 6>>
```

Erlang supports matching binaries with size specifications, useful when dealing with data that does not align perfectly with byte boundaries.

```
% Matching with non-byte-aligned sizes
<<X:4, Y:4, Z:8>> = <<15, 16, 255>>.
```

In this case:

```
X = 15,
Y = 1,
Z = 255
```

Binary Comprehensions

Binary comprehensions simplify the processing and transformation of binary data. They operate similarly to list comprehensions but are optimized for binaries.

```
% Binary comprehension example
List = [1, 2, 3, 4],
Binary = << <<X:8>> || X <- List >>.
```

This comprehension converts a list of numbers into a binary, where each list element is an 8-bit segment of the resulting binary.

Binary Construction

Constructing binaries efficiently is important for performance-sensitive applications. Erlang's binary syntax supports various techniques to build binaries without unnecessary copying.

```
% Binary construction using list of binaries
Binaries = [<<1>>, <<2>>, <<3>>],
Result = <<(<< <<Bin/binary>> || Bin <- Binaries >>)>>.
```

This example concatenates a list of binaries into a single binary using a binary comprehension.

Optimizing Binaries for Efficiency

Efficiency considerations for binary data handling involve minimizing memory copying and fragmentation. Erlang uses a concept called sub-binaries to reference slices of existing binaries without duplicating the data.

```
% Creating a sub-binary
Original = <<1, 2, 3, 4, 5, 6>>,
Sub = binary:part(Original, 2, 3).
```

Sub references the part of Original starting at byte position 2 with a length of 3 bytes.

```
Sub = <<3, 4, 5>>
```

Managing large binaries efficiently requires understanding Erlang's garbage collection behavior, as large binaries are allocated outside the process heap. Each binary is reference-counted and shared across processes unless explicitly copied.

Binary Module Functions

Erlang's binary module offers a range of functions for binary manipulation, including binary:split/2, binary:match/2, and binary:replace/3. These functions facilitate common binary operations like splitting, searching, and replacing binary segments.

```
% Splitting a binary
Parts = binary:split(<<1, 2, 3, 4, 5, 6>>, <<3>>).
```

This splits the binary at the byte 3, resulting in a list of binaries.

```
Parts = [<<1, 2>>, <<4, 5, 6>>]
```

binary:match/2 searches for a pattern within a binary and returns the position.

```
% Searching within a binary
Position = binary:match(<<1, 2, 3, 4, 5>>, <<3>>).
```

Position = {match, 3}

binary:replace/3 replaces occurrences of a pattern in a binary with another binary.

```
% Replacing bytes in a binary
NewBin = binary:replace(<<1, 2, 3>>, <<2>>, <<99>>).
```

NewBin = <<1, 99, 3>>

These functions and constructs enable comprehensive and efficient manipulation of binary data in Erlang, essential for applications demanding precise control over data representation and processing efficiency.

4.8 Data Structure Efficiency

Understanding the efficiency of data structures is critical in optimizing Erlang programs. This section analyzes the time and space complexities associated with lists, tuples, maps, records, sets, and binary data structures. Efficiency considerations are paramount in high-performance systems where computing resources and response times are critical.

Lists: Time and Space Complexity

Lists in Erlang are implemented as singly linked lists. Each element contains the data and a reference to the next element. The implications of this implementation include:

- **Access Time:** Accessing the head of the list is $O(1)$ since it involves a single reference. However, accessing an element at position n in the list requires $O(n)$ time.
- **Insertion Time:** Insertion at the head is $O(1)$, while insertion at position n is $O(n)$.
- **Deletion Time:** Removing the head is $O(1)$, but removing an element from position n takes $O(n)$ time.
- **Space Complexity:** Each element requires memory for the data and a reference pointer, resulting in a linear space requirement of $O(n)$.

```
% Example for accessing the head of the list
List = [3, 5, 7, 9],
Hd = hd(List). % Operation is O(1)
```

3

Tuples: Time and Space Complexity

Tuples in Erlang are a fixed-size collection of elements. They differ markedly from lists in their performance characteristics:

- **Access Time:** Accessing an element by its index is $O(1)$ due to the direct indexing.
- **Insertion and Deletion Time:** Tuples are immutable, so insertion or deletion requires creating a new tuple, resulting in $O(n)$ time where n is the size of the tuple.
- **Space Complexity:** Since tuples are contiguous in memory, the space required is linear, $O(n)$, where n is the number of elements.

```
% Example for accessing the first element of the tuple
Tuple = {1, 2, 3, 4},
FirstElement = element(1, Tuple). % Operation is O(1)
```

1

Maps: Time and Space Complexity

Maps in Erlang are used for key-value storage and provide more flexibility than lists and tuples:

- **Access Time:** Accessing a value by its key can be considered $O(\log n)$ on average.
- **Insertion and Deletion Time:** Adding or removing a key-value pair also takes $O(\log n)$.
- **Space Complexity:** The space requirement is linear, $O(n)$, accounting for the keys and values.

```
% Example for accessing a value by its key
Map = #{name => "Alice", age => 30},
Age = maps:get(age, Map). % Operation is O(log n)
```

30

Records: Time and Space Complexity

Records in Erlang offer a convenient way to store structured data. Internally, records are tuples with named fields. The performance characteristics inherit from tuples:

- **Access Time:** Accessing a field is $O(1)$ since it's based on tuple indexing.
- **Insertion and Deletion Time:** As with tuples, modification requires creating a new record, leading to $O(n)$ time.
- **Space Complexity:** Linear space, $O(n)$, where n is the number of fields.

```
-record(person, {name, age}).
% Example for creating and accessing a record field
P = #person{name="Bob", age=21},
Name = P#person.name. % Operation is O(1)
```

```
Bob
```

Sets: Time and Space Complexity

Sets in Erlang are used to maintain a collection of unique elements, with the following characteristics:

- **Access Time:** Checking membership or accessing an element can be done in $O(\log n)$ average time.
- **Insertion and Deletion Time:** Adding or removing elements also takes $O(\log n)$ average time.
- **Space Complexity:** Linear space requirement, $O(n)$.

```
% Example for adding an element to a set
Set1 = sets:add_element(10, sets:new()),
Set2 = sets:add_element(20, Set1).
HappyPath = sets:is_element(10, Set2). % Operation is O(log n)
```

```
true
```

Binary Data: Time and Space Complexity

Handling binary data efficiently is crucial in Erlang, especially for applications involving extensive data transmission or processing. Binaries in Erlang are optimally engineered for size and performance.

- **Access Time:** Accessing parts of the binary data is $O(1)$ using pattern matching.

- **Insertion and Deletion Time:** Operations involving concatenation or segmentation necessitate copying and can be $O(n)$.
- **Space Complexity:** Binaries offer efficient space utilization due to their compact representation, typically requiring $O(n)$ space.

```
% Example for accessing parts of binary data
Bin = <<1, 2, 3, 4, 5>>,
<<First, Rest/bytes>> = Bin. % Operation is O(1)
```

```
1
<<2,3,4,5>>
```

Special care must be taken to select the appropriate data structure based on the required operations and performance considerations to ensure that the program executes efficiently and within resource constraints.

Chapter 5

Concurrent Programming in Erlang

This chapter explores concurrent programming in Erlang, beginning with an introduction to concurrency and the actor model. It covers creating and managing processes, message passing, synchronization, and coordination. Additionally, the chapter addresses process monitoring and linking, error handling in concurrent systems, and common design patterns for concurrency, providing a solid foundation for effective concurrent programming in Erlang.

5.1 Introduction to Concurrency in Erlang

Concurrency is an integral aspect of Erlang's design, providing the capacity to perform multiple operations in parallel. This capability is particularly well-suited for developing distributed and fault-tolerant systems. Erlang employs the actor model of concurrency, where 'actors' are the fundamental units that interact through message passing, avoiding shared state and locks that are typical in traditional concurrent programming.

Erlang's concurrency model is lightweight, enabling the creation of thousands of concurrent processes without significant overhead. Each Erlang process has its own heap and stack and is scheduled by the Erlang runtime system (ERTS). Unlike OS-level threads, Erlang processes are managed by the ERTS, leading to more efficient context switching and better resource utilization.

```
% Example of creating a simple process in Erlang
-module(concurrency_example).
-export([start/0, loop/0]).

start() ->
    Pid = spawn(fun loop/0),
    Pid ! {self(), "Hello, process!"}.

loop() ->
    receive
        {From, Msg} ->
            io:format("Received ~p from ~p~n", [Msg, From]),
            From ! ok,
            loop()
    end.
```

In this example, the start/0 function creates a new process by calling the spawn/1 function. The newly created process runs the loop/0 function. This process waits for a message in its mailbox and processes it using the receive block. When it receives a message, it outputs the message and the sender's process id, replies with an ok message to the sender, and recursively calls loop/0 to wait for the next message.

An essential element of Erlang's concurrency model is the message passing mechanism, enabling processes to communicate without shared memory. Messages are delivered asynchronously, and the receive block is used to extract messages from a process's mailbox. This method ensures data isolation and helps avoid race conditions, a common problem in concurrent programming.

```
% Expected output from the concurrency_example module
Received "Hello, process!" from <0.42.0>
```

Process scheduling in Erlang is preemptive, ensuring that each process gets a share of processing time. The Erlang scheduler uses a reduction-based scheduling mechanism, where a process is allowed to run for a fixed number of reductions (function calls or message processing steps) before it is preempted. This approach ensures fairness and responsiveness in a system with numerous processes.

```
% Illustration of message passing mechanism
-module(message_passing).
-export([send_message/2, receive_message/0]).

send_message(Pid, Msg) ->
    Pid ! {self(), Msg}.
```

```
receive_message() ->
    receive
        {From, Msg} ->
            io:format("Message ~p received from ~p~n", [Msg, From])
    end.
```

Here, send_message/2 sends a message Msg to the process identified by Pid. The message includes the sender's process identifier (self()) and the message content. The receive_message/0 function waits for a message and, upon receiving it, prints the message and the sender's information.

The lightweight nature of Erlang processes is achieved through the **Erlang runtime system's** ability to efficiently manage process creation, execution, and termination. This efficiency is crucial for building systems that require high levels of concurrency, such as telecommunication switches, real-time control systems, and web servers.

Error handling in Erlang's concurrent systems follows the "let it crash" philosophy, wherein processes are designed to fail independently without affecting the entire system. This fault tolerance is facilitated by process linking and monitoring, enabling processes to detect failures and take corrective actions.

Efficient concurrent programming in Erlang necessitates a solid understanding of **process lifecycle**, message passing, and scheduling. Mastering these concepts enables developers to leverage Erlang's powerful concurrency model and build robust, fault-tolerant applications.

5.2 The Actor Model

The actor model serves as the foundational concept for concurrency in Erlang. It envisions a system of independent actors which interact by exchanging messages. Each actor handles its own state and lifecycle, promoting a clear separation of concerns and simplifying the synchronization mechanisms.

An actor, fundamentally, is an entity that:

- Has a unique address or identifier.
- Can receive messages from other actors.
- Processes received messages one at a time.

- Can send messages to other actors.
- Can create new actors.

This architecture avoids the shared memory paradigm, thus eliminating the complexities and potential issues of race conditions and deadlocks inherent in traditional multithreading approaches. Instead, actors communicate asynchronously, ensuring safe and efficient concurrency.

Creating and Managing Actors

In Erlang, actors are represented by processes. Each process runs independently and concurrently with its own state. Processes in Erlang are lightweight, enabling the system to handle thousands or even millions of concurrent processes efficiently.

To create a new process, the spawn function is used. The basic syntax is:

```
Pid = spawn(Module, Function, Args)
```

Here, Module is the module name where the function resides, Function is the name of the function to be executed by the new process, and Args is a list of arguments to be passed to the function.

Consider an example where we create a simple actor that prints a message:

```
-module(actor_example).
-export([start/0, loop/0]).

start() ->
    spawn(?MODULE, loop, []).

loop() ->
    receive
        {print_msg, Msg} ->
            io:format("Message received: ~p~n", [Msg]),
            loop(); % Recursively call loop to handle more messages
        stop ->
            ok % End the loop and terminate the process
    end.
```

To start this actor and send a message, we can use:

```
1> actor_example:start().
<0.34.0>
2> Pid = actor_example:start().
<0.35.0>
3> Pid ! {print_msg, "Hello, Actor!"}.
Message received: "Hello, Actor!"
{print_msg,"Hello, Actor!"}
4> Pid ! stop.
stop
```

```
% 1> Starts the actor but does not retain the PID
% 2> Starts another actor and retains its PID
% 3> Sends a message to the second started actor
% 4> Sends a stop message to the second started actor
```

Message Passing

Message passing between actors is performed using the ! (send operator). Any value can be sent as a message, and the recipient processes these messages in the order they arrive. Processes handle these messages within a receive block.

A more complex example can involve actors performing computations. Let's illustrate an actor that computes the factorial of a number:

```
-module(factorial_actor).
-export([start/0, factorial/0]).

start() ->
    spawn(?MODULE, factorial, []).

factorial() ->
    receive
        {compute, N, Sender} when is_integer(N), N >= 0 ->
            Sender ! {result, self(), fac(N)},
            factorial();
        stop ->
            ok
    end.

fac(0) -> 1;
fac(N) -> N * fac(N - 1).
```

To request a factorial computation and receive the result, another process can interact with factorial_actor as follows:

```
1> Pid = factorial_actor:start().
<0.36.0>
2> Pid ! {compute, 5, self()}.
{compute,5,<0.32.0>}
3> receive
    {result, Pid, Result} ->
        io:format("Factorial result: ~p~n", [Result])
  end.
Factorial result: 120
```

```
% 1> Start the factorial actor and retain its PID
% 2> Send a compute message to the actor, specifying the number and our PID for the result
% 3> Wait and process the result when it arrives, printing it out
```

Fault Tolerance

Erlang's actor model inherently supports fault tolerance via process monitoring and linking. Fault tolerance is achieved using spawn_link and monitor mechanisms. When a process is linked to another, if one fails, the other is notified and can take corrective action.

Consider a simple supervisor example:

```
-module(supervisor_example).
-export([start/0, init/0, supervise/2]).

start() ->
    spawn_link(?MODULE, init, []).

init() ->
    Child = spawn_link(?MODULE, child_process, []),
    supervise(Child, 0).

supervise(Child, RestartCount) when RestartCount < 3 ->
    receive
        {'EXIT', Child, Reason} ->
            io:format("Child process terminated: ~p~n", [Reason]),
            NewChild = spawn_link(?MODULE, child_process, []),
            supervise(NewChild, RestartCount + 1)
    end;
supervise(_, _) ->
    io:format("Child process reached restart limit~n").

child_process() ->
    exit(die).
```

Running the supervisor demonstrates automatic restarting of the child process until a limit is reached:

```
1> supervisor_example:start().
Child process terminated: die
Child process terminated: die
Child process terminated: die
Child process reached restart limit
```

% 1> Start the supervisor and observe child process restarts. After three restarts, the process terminates

An actor-based concurrent system in Erlang promotes robustness, maintainability, and scalability. By isolating process states and interactions, Erlang effectively manages concurrent operations with minimal overhead.

5.3 Creating and Managing Processes

Creating and managing processes in Erlang is a fundamental aspect of leveraging its concurrency capabilities. Erlang employs lightweight processes which are managed by the BEAM virtual machine. This section delves into the mechanisms to create, manage, and control these processes, focusing on practical implementation and nuances.

The spawn function is the primary mechanism for creating processes in Erlang. It can be utilized in various forms to suit different requirements.

spawn/1 creates a process by invoking a zero-arity function (a function with no arguments):

```
spawn(fun() -> io:format("Hello from the new process!~n") end).
```

spawn/2 and spawn/3 provide more control by allowing the specification of the module, function, and arguments to be passed to the function. By way of illustration:

```
% spawn/3 creates a process to run the my_function in the my_module with
      arguments Arg1 and Arg2
spawn(my_module, my_function, [Arg1, Arg2]).
```

Each call to spawn returns a pid, a unique process identifier, which can be used to interact with the newly created process.

```
% Example of retrieving the Pid of the spawned process
Pid = spawn(fun() -> io:format("Process ~p started~n", [self()]) end).
```

Processes in Erlang do not share memory. They communicate by sending messages to each other's mailboxes. The self/0 function returns the pid of the calling process, facilitating easier sending and receiving of messages.

```
% Example of process interaction using message passing
Pid = spawn(fun() -> receive
                        {msg, Text} -> io:format("Received: ~s~n", [Text])
                     end
            end).

% Sending a message to the PID of the spawned process
Pid ! {msg, "Hello, Process!"}.
```

A process can be terminated using the exit/1 or exit/2 function. The exit/1 function terminates the calling process, while exit/2 can be used to terminate another process by sending an exit signal along with a reason.

```
% Using exit/1 to terminate the current process
exit(normal).

% Using exit/2 to terminate another process
exit(Pid, kill).
```

Processes manage termination signals through links. By linking two processes, they can monitor each other's termination. Linking is done using the link/1 function. If a linked process terminates unexpectedly, it sends an exit signal to all linked processes.

```
% Example of two-way linkage between processes
Pid1 = spawn(fun() -> process_flag(trap_exit, true),
```

```
            receive
                {'EXIT', From, Reason} ->
                    io:format("Process ~p terminated with reason: ~p~n",
                              [From, Reason])
            end
    end).
Pid2 = spawn_link(fun() -> io:format("Process ~p started~n", [self()]),
            exit(Pid1, kill) end).
```

Unidirectional monitoring can be achieved using the monitor/1 function, which returns a reference that can capture termination messages of the monitored process.

```
% Example of monitoring another process
Ref = erlang:monitor(process, Pid),
Pid = spawn(fun() -> receive
                {'DOWN', Ref1, process, Pid, Reason} ->
                    io:format("Monitored process ~p terminated with
                        reason: ~p~n", [Pid, Reason])
        end
        end).
```

The demonitor/1 function is used to stop monitoring a process. This is essential to avoid keeping unnecessary state or receiving unexpected messages.

```
% Stop monitoring the Pid
erlang:demonitor(Ref, [flush]).
```

Erlang also incorporates the use of process dictionaries, which allow processes to store state. This is useful for certain design patterns. The put/2 and get/1 functions access the process dictionary.

```
% Storing and retrieving values in a process dictionary
put(key, "value").
Value = get(key).
```

Finally, managing processes effectively requires understanding different process states and corresponding changes. Using the aforementioned practices ensures robust and efficient concurrent applications.

5.4 Message Passing

In Erlang, message passing is the primary mechanism for communication between processes. This section delves into the fundamental aspects of message passing, focusing on the underlying principles, syntax, and practical usage in concurrent programming.

The foundation of message passing in Erlang lies in its use of the actor model, where each process is an independent entity capable of sending and receiving messages asynchronously. This paradigm allows for a high degree of concurrency, scalability, and fault tolerance.

Sending Messages

Messages are sent using the ! operator, which is used to send a message to a process's mailbox. The general syntax is:

```
Pid ! Message
```

Here, Pid is the process identifier of the recipient, and Message is the data being sent. The Message can be any Erlang term, such as atoms, tuples, lists, or more complex structures.

Consider the following example:

```
process_example() ->
    Pid = spawn(fun() -> receive_message() end),
    Pid ! {self(), "Hello, Erlang"}.

receive_message() ->
    receive
        {Sender, Message} ->
            io:format("Received ~p from ~p~n", [Message, Sender])
    end.
```

In this example, a new process is spawned, executing the receive_message/0 function. The parent process sends a message to the child process containing its own Pid and a greeting string. The child process then uses a receive block to handle incoming messages.

Receiving Messages

Erlang processes check their mailboxes for incoming messages using the receive construct. The receive block allows a process to specify patterns to match incoming messages and execute corresponding actions. The basic form is:

```
receive
    Pattern1 ->
        Actions1;
    Pattern2 ->
        Actions2;
    ...
    PatternN ->
        ActionsN
end
```

Each Pattern is a pattern that matches the incoming message, and its corresponding Actions are executed if the pattern matches. If no pattern matches the current message, it remains in the mailbox, and the process continues waiting for a matching message.

Selective Receive

Erlang's receive block inherently supports selective receive, allowing processes to handle messages out of order based on their patterns. This capability is vital for implementing sophisticated communication protocols and handling multiple message types.

Consider a process that needs to handle different types of messages:

```
handle_messages() ->
    receive
        {compute, Data} ->
            Result = perform_computation(Data),
            io:format("Computed result: ~p~n", [Result]);
        {log, Message} ->
            io:format("Log: ~s~n", [Message]);
        exit ->
            io:format("Exiting~n"),
            exit(normal)
    end,
    handle_messages().
```

In this example, the process can handle computation requests, log messages, and exit commands. The handle_messages/0 function is recursive, allowing the process to continue handling messages indefinitely.

Timeouts in Message Passing

Erlang's receive block can be augmented with timeouts, providing a mechanism to handle cases where no message arrives within a specified time frame. This is useful for implementing response timeouts, retry mechanisms, and other time-sensitive behaviors.

The syntax for adding a timeout is as follows:

```
receive
    Pattern1 ->
        Actions1;
    Pattern2 ->
        Actions2;
    ...
    after Timeout ->
        TimeoutActions
end
```

Here, Timeout specifies the time in milliseconds, and TimeoutActions are executed if no message matches the patterns before the timeout period elapses.

For instance:

```
handle_request() ->
    receive
        {request, Data} ->
            io:format("Handling request: ~p~n", [Data]);
        after 5000 ->
            io:format("Request timed out~n")
    end.
```

In this example, if no request message is received within 5 seconds, a timeout message is printed.

Buffering and Order of Messages

Messages sent to an Erlang process are stored in its mailbox. Messages are retrieved from the mailbox using a receive block, which processes them in the order they arrive unless selective receive is used.

It is important to note that while message order is preserved for messages sent by the same process, there is no guarantee about the order of messages sent by multiple processes. This ensures that concurrency does not introduce timing-related issues, but developers need to be mindful of potential message reordering when designing concurrent systems.

Pattern Matching in Message Passing

Pattern matching is a powerful feature in Erlang message passing, allowing processes to filter and handle messages efficiently. The structure and content of messages can be matched against patterns, facilitating the implementation of complex protocols and data processing pipelines.

Consider a scenario where a process handles different commands and requests:

```
command_handler() ->
    receive
        {command, {operation, Op}, {operand1, X}, {operand2, Y}} ->
            Result = execute_command(Op, X, Y),
            io:format("Command result: ~p~n", [Result]);
        {query, Info} ->
            Response = process_query(Info),
            io:format("Query response: ~p~n", [Response])
    end.
```

In this example, the process distinguishes between command messages and query messages, extracting relevant data through pattern matching and performing the appropriate actions.

Avoiding Common Pitfalls in Message Passing

While message passing in Erlang is straightforward, certain pitfalls can arise, particularly in large or complex systems. One common issue is the accumulation of unprocessed messages in a process's mailbox, leading to memory bloat and decreased performance. To mitigate this, ensure that processes handle messages promptly and efficiently.

Another potential issue is the inadvertent pattern matching of unrelated messages, which can lead to unexpected behaviors. To avoid this, carefully design message patterns and avoid overly generic matches.

Understanding and mastering message passing in Erlang is crucial for effective concurrent programming, enabling developers to build responsive, resilient, and scalable systems.

5.5 Synchronization and Coordination

In concurrent programming, synchronization and coordination are crucial to ensuring that processes work correctly when they need to share data or resources. Erlang provides several mechanisms and constructs to facilitate synchronization and coordination between processes. This section elaborates on these mechanisms, illustrating their use and discussing potential pitfalls.

Message Ordering Guarantees

Erlang guarantees that if process P_1 sends multiple messages to process P_2, those messages will arrive in the order they were sent. However, there is no guarantee that messages sent by different processes will arrive in any particular order. This foundational principle of message passing in Erlang ensures that processes can rely on the order of messages they receive, a key aspect of synchronization.

```
% Process 1
P2 ! {self(), msg1},
P2 ! {self(), msg2}

% Process 2
receive
    {P1, msg1} ->
        %% handle msg1
        receive
            {P1, msg2} ->
                %% handle msg2
        end
end.
```

Here, msg1 will be received by P2 before msg2 as sent by P1.

Selective Receive

Selective receive allows a process to pick specific messages from its mailbox based on patterns, enabling synchronization by waiting for particular messages. While this provides flexibility, improper use can lead to complex and hard-to-debug systems.

```
receive
    {P1, Data} ->
        %% handle data from P1
after
    5000 ->
        %% handle timeout
end.
```

In this scenario, the process handles messages only from P1. If no such message arrives within 5000 milliseconds, it handles a timeout scenario.

Synchronization with Monitors and Links

Monitors and links are used to manage dependencies and synchronize termination between processes.

Using Monitors: A monitor allows a process to keep track of another process's status without creating bidirectional dependencies.

```
%% Process A
MonitorRef = erlang:monitor(process, PidB).

%% Process B
exit(PidB, normal).

%% Process A receiving the 'DOWN' message
receive
    {'DOWN', MonitorRef, process, PidB, Reason} ->
        %% handle PidB's termination
end.
```

Here, MonitorRef is a reference to the monitor created. The message {'DOWN', MonitorRef, process, PidB, Reason} notifies Process A of PidB's termination, synchronizing Process A's actions accordingly.

Using Links: Links create a bidirectional connection where the failure of one process can lead to the termination of the linked process unless it's trapping exits.

```
%% Process A
```

```
link(PidB).

%% Process B
exit(PidB, normal).

%% Process A in case it's trapping exits
process_flag(trap_exit, true),
receive
    {'EXIT', PidB, Reason} ->
        %% handle PidB's termination
end.
```

This mechanism ensures that linked processes can take necessary actions, such as clean-up, on termination, providing another form of coordination.

Global Synchronization

For scenarios requiring multiple processes to synchronize on a common event, Erlang's gen_server and other behaviors provide robust abstractions. A gen_server can manage state and synchronize actions of multiple clients.

```
%% Example gen_server
-module(synch_server).
-behaviour(gen_server).

%% Callbacks
init([]) ->
    {ok, #{}}.

handle_call({sync, Data}, _From, State) ->
    %% synchronize on Data
    {reply, ok, State};

%% Other callbacks
...
```

Clients interact with synch_server via synchronous calls, ensuring serialized access to shared resources and consistent state updates.

Handling Synchronized State with ETS

Erlang Term Storage (ETS) is a powerful in-memory storage system providing fast read/write access to concurrent processes.

```
%% Create an ETS table
TableRef = ets:new(my_table, [named_table, set, public]).

%% Insert data
ets:insert(my_table, {Key, Value}).
```

```
%% Lookup data
case ets:lookup(my_table, Key) of
    [] -> %% Key not found
        ...
    [{Key, Value}] -> %% Key found
        ...
end.
```

ETS tables offer an effective means for processes to synchronize data access and modifications efficiently, reducing the intricacies of message-based synchronization.

```
Output:
ok
{key, value}
```

Effective synchronization and coordination are critical for maintaining data integrity and process-aware actions in concurrent systems. By leveraging message ordering guarantees, selective receive, monitors, links, gen_server, and ETS, Erlang provides robust tools to design reliable concurrent applications.

5.6 Process Monitoring and Linking

Process monitoring and linking are essential mechanisms in Erlang for building robust concurrent systems. Understanding these mechanisms allows you to effectively manage process lifecycles and handle faults gracefully.

Process Monitoring

Monitoring a process provides a way to keep track of its status and receive notifications if the process terminates, whether normally or due to an error. The erlang:monitor/2 function is used to create such a monitoring relationship. The basic syntax is as follows:

```
MonitorRef = erlang:monitor(process, Pid).
```

Here, Pid refers to the process identifier of the process to be monitored. The MonitorRef is a unique reference that can be used to identify the monitoring relationship.

When the monitored process terminates, a 'DOWN' message is sent to the monitoring process. The structure of this message is:

```
{'DOWN', MonitorRef, process, Pid, Reason}
```

Where:

- MonitorRef is the reference created by erlang:monitor/2.
- Pid is the identifier of the terminated process.
- Reason describes why the process terminated and can be normal, an error reason, or killed.

Consider the following example in which a process monitors another process:

```
start_monitoring() ->
    Pid = spawn(fun() -> some_work() end),
    MonitorRef = erlang:monitor(process, Pid),
    receive
        {'DOWN', MonitorRef, process, Pid, Reason} ->
            io:format("Process ~p terminated with reason ~p~n", [Pid, Reason])
    end.

some_work() ->
    %% Simulate some work
    timer:sleep(5000).
```

In this example, a process is created and monitored. The monitoring process will wait to receive a 'DOWN' message when the monitored process completes its work and terminates.

Process Linking

Linking processes is another fundamental concept in Erlang that creates a bidirectional relationship between processes. When processes are linked, if one process terminates, the other linked processes receive an 'EXIT' signal. This is done using the link/1 function:

```
erlang:link(Pid).
```

If a process crashes, all linked processes will also terminate unless they are trapping exits. A process can trap exits by setting the process_flag(trap_exit, true) flag, which converts 'EXIT' signals into messages that can be handled explicitly.

```
trap_and_link() ->
    process_flag(trap_exit, true),
    Pid = spawn_link(fun() -> error(prone_function()) end),
    receive
        {'EXIT', Pid, Reason} ->
            io:format("Linked process ~p exited with reason ~p~n", [Pid, Reason])
    end.

prone_function() ->
    %% Simulate an error
    exit(badarg).
```

In this code, a process sets its trap_exit flag to true and spawns a linked process. If the linked process exits with an error, the parent process receives an 'EXIT' message instead of terminating.

Comparing Monitoring and Linking

While both monitoring and linking are used to observe process terminations, they serve different purposes and have distinct characteristics:

- Monitoring is unidirectional; the monitoring process receives 'DOWN' messages about the monitored process's status, but the monitored process is unaffected if the monitoring process terminates.
- Linking is bidirectional; both linked processes are notified if either process terminates, causing a chain reaction unless exits are trapped.
- Monitoring can be used across nodes in a distributed system, whereas Linking is more appropriate within a single node to manage fault propagation.

Using these mechanisms, you can ensure better supervision and control of concurrent processes. Choosing between monitoring and linking depends on the specific requirements of your system's fault tolerance and behavior.

Practical Use Case: Supervisor Behavior

In practice, these concepts are encapsulated in Erlang's OTP framework through the supervisor behavior. A supervisor process is designed to monitor and manage worker processes, restarting them when necessary. The following is a simplified supervisor implementation:

```
-module(simple_supervisor).
-behaviour(supervisor).

-export([start_link/0, init/1]).

start_link() ->
    supervisor:start_link({local, ?MODULE}, ?MODULE, []).

init([]) ->
    SupFlags = #{strategy => one_for_one, intensity => 1, period => 5},
    ChildSpecs = [
        #{id => worker, start => {worker_module, start_link, []},
          restart => permanent, shutdown => 2000, type => worker}
    ],
    {ok, {SupFlags, ChildSpecs}}.
```

Here, simple_supervisor defines a supervisor that starts a worker child process. The supervisor uses the one_for_one strategy, meaning each worker is supervised individually and restarted upon failure.

By leveraging monitoring, linking, and the supervisor behavior, one can design resilient systems that gracefully handle process failures, ensuring the robustness and reliability critical to concurrent programming in Erlang.

5.7 Error Handling in Concurrent Systems

Error handling in concurrent systems is a critical aspect of building robust and resilient applications in Erlang. This section focuses on the mechanisms and strategies employed for handling errors effectively, ensuring that the system can recover from faults and continue operating reliably. By leveraging Erlang's unique capabilities, developers can create systems that maintain high availability and reliability even in the presence of errors.

Linking Processes

One fundamental concept in Erlang for error handling is linking processes. When processes are linked, they create a bidirectional relationship, meaning that if one process terminates, the linked process will also receive an exit signal. This mechanism allows for the coordinated shutdown of related processes, ensuring that failures are contained and managed.

```
%% Example: Linking two processes
Pid1 = spawn(fun() -> loop() end),
Pid2 = spawn(fun() -> loop() end),
link(Pid1),
link(Pid2),
```

In the example above, Pid1 and Pid2 are linked. If either process terminates, the other process will be notified and can take appropriate action.

Trap Exit Signals

Erlang processes can handle exit signals from linked processes by trapping exits. By setting a process flag, a process can convert exit signals into messages, allowing it to handle the exit of linked processes gracefully.

```
%% Enabling trap exit in a process
```

```
process_flag(trap_exit, true),

%% Handling exit signals in the receive block
receive
    {'EXIT', From, Reason} ->
        %% Handle the exit notification
        io:format("Process ~p exited with reason ~p~n", [From, Reason]);
    Other ->
        %% Handle other messages
        io:format("Received message: ~p~n", [Other])
end,
```

In this code snippet, the process sets the trap_exit flag to true, enabling it to receive exit signals as messages in its receive block. By handling the 'EXIT' message, the process can perform necessary cleanup or recovery actions.

Supervision Trees

A cornerstone of Erlang's error-handling strategy is the use of supervision trees. A supervision tree is a hierarchical structure in which supervisor processes oversee worker processes, managing their lifecycle and recovering from failures. Supervisors are configured with a strategy for handling child process terminations, such as restarting the failed processes.

```
%% Defining a simple supervisor
-module(simple_supervisor).
-behaviour(supervisor).

%% Supervisor specification
init([]) ->
    {ok, {{one_for_one, 5, 10},
          [{worker1, {worker_module, start_link, []}, permanent, brutal_kill, worker, [
              worker_module]},
           {worker2, {worker_module, start_link, []}, permanent, brutal_kill, worker, [
              worker_module]}]}}.

%% Start the supervisor
start_supervisor() ->
  supervisor:start_link({local, ?MODULE}, ?MODULE, []).
```

In this example, a supervisor is defined with two worker processes. The supervisor uses the one_for_one strategy, meaning that if a worker process terminates, only that specific worker will be restarted. Various restart strategies and intensity limits can be configured to suit different use cases.

Error Logging and Diagnostics

Effective error handling also involves logging errors and diagnostics. Erlang provides built-in tools for logging and diagnostics to help identify and resolve issues in concurrent systems. The error_logger and dbg modules are commonly used for this purpose.

```
%% Logging an error message
error_logger:error_msg("Error occurred: ~p", [Reason]),

%% Using dbg for tracing messages
dbg:tracer(),
dbg:p(all, [all]),
dbg:tpl(Module, Function, arity, []),
```

In this example, the error_logger:error_msg/2 function logs an error message with the specified Reason. The dbg module is used to set up tracing, allowing developers to trace function calls and messages for deeper diagnostics.

Best Practices for Error Handling

When designing error handling for concurrent systems in Erlang, the following best practices should be considered:

- **Isolate Errors**: Design processes to handle their own errors and fail independently, preventing cascading failures.
- **Leverage Supervisors**: Utilize supervision trees to manage process lifecycles and recovery, ensuring fault containment.
- **Use Trap Exit Sparingly**: Trap exits only when necessary, as excessive use can complicate error handling and recovery.
- **Log and Monitor**: Implement logging and monitoring to detect and diagnose errors promptly, facilitating quick resolution.
- **Test Error Scenarios**: Regularly test error scenarios to ensure the system behaves as expected under failure conditions.

By adhering to these practices, developers can effectively manage errors in concurrent systems, achieving robust and resilient applications.

5.8 Design Patterns for Concurrency

This section delves into various design patterns pivotal for effective concurrent programming in Erlang. Patterns are essential as they encapsulate proven solutions to common problems encountered in concurrent programming, promoting code reuse, readability, and maintainability. We will discuss several fundamental concurrency patterns, including the Supervisor, Worker Pool, and Events and Handlers patterns.

Supervisor Pattern

The Supervisor pattern is central to Erlang's fault-tolerant design. Supervisors are processes designed to monitor and manage other processes, known as worker processes. Supervisors can restart failed workers based on predefined strategies, ensuring system robustness.

In Erlang, a Supervisor is typically implemented using the OTP supervisor behavior. Consider the implementation below:

```
-module(simple_supervisor).
-behaviour(supervisor).

%% API
-export([start_link/0]).

%% Supervisor callbacks
-export([init/1]).

start_link() ->
    supervisor:start_link({local, ?MODULE}, ?MODULE, []).

init([]) ->
    {ok, { {one_for_one, 5, 10},
           [
               {worker_one, {worker_one, start_link, []}, permanent, brutal_kill,
                   worker, [worker_one]}
           ]
         }
    }.
```

In this example, the simple_supervisor module defines a supervisor that manages a single worker process named worker_one. The restart strategy one_for_one ensures that if worker_one fails, only worker_one is restarted.

Worker Pool Pattern

The Worker Pool pattern is used to manage a pool of worker processes to perform tasks concurrently. This pattern is beneficial for distributing workloads efficiently and balancing across multiple processes.

The following example demonstrates a basic worker pool implementation in Erlang:

```
-module(worker_pool).
-export([start_link/2, submit_task/2]).

start_link(NumWorkers, WorkerModule) ->
    Pool = lists:map(fun(_) -> start_worker(WorkerModule) end, lists:seq(1,
           NumWorkers)),
    {ok, Pool}.

start_worker(WorkerModule) ->
    {ok, Pid} = WorkerModule:start_link(),
    Pid.
```

```
submit_task(Pool, Task) ->
    Worker = lists:nth(rand:uniform(length(Pool)), Pool),
    Worker ! Task.
```

In this implementation, the start_link/2 function initializes a fixed number of worker processes from the WorkerModule. The submit_task/2 function selects a random worker from the pool to handle the incoming Task.

Events and Handlers Pattern

The Events and Handlers pattern involves decoupling event generation from event handling. This pattern is particularly useful for building scalable systems where multiple handlers may process events asynchronously.

Consider the following example:

```
-module(event_manager).
-export([start_link/2, notify_event/2, register_handler/2]).

start_link() ->
    {ok, spawn(fun loop/0)}.

register_handler(Pid, Handler) ->
    Pid ! {register_handler, Handler}.

notify_event(Pid, Event) ->
    Pid ! {notify_event, Event}.

loop() ->
    receive
        {register_handler, Handler} ->
            loop([Handler]);
        {notify_event, Event} ->
            handle_event([Handler], Event),
            loop()
    end.

handle_event([], _) -> ok;
handle_event([H|T], Event) ->
    H ! Event,
    handle_event(T, Event).
```

Here, the event_manager module facilitates registering handlers and notifying events. The loop/1 function maintains a list of handlers and dispatches events to all registered handlers.

Delving into these patterns reveals how they can be synergistically combined for building resilient, scalable concurrent systems. Each design pattern addresses specific aspects of concurrency, and by applying them appropriately, developers can harness the full power of Erlang's concurrency model.

Chapter 6

Error Handling and Fault Tolerance

This chapter addresses error handling and fault tolerance in Erlang, starting with the philosophy behind Erlang's approach. It covers exceptions and error handling mechanisms, process supervision, and the use of supervision trees. Additionally, the chapter discusses creating and managing workers, fault tolerance strategies, logging, monitoring, and presents case studies to illustrate effective fault-tolerant system design in Erlang.

6.1 Philosophy of Error Handling in Erlang

Erlang's approach to error handling is fundamentally different from many other programming languages. Traditional languages often emphasize catching and handling errors locally, aiming for stability within individual modules or classes. In contrast, Erlang adopts a fail-fast philosophy, promoting the quick detection and propagation of errors to higher-level supervisors. This approach is rooted in several core principles that are integral to building robust, fault-tolerant systems.

Let It Crash is one of the cornerstone philosophies of Erlang. Rather than trying to meticulously handle all potential errors within each function, Erlang encourages developers to focus on writing correct code under normal operations and let processes crash if they encounter unexpected conditions. This is largely facilitated by Erlang's lightweight process model, where processes are isolated from one another and failures do not propagate, thus containing any potential system-wide disruption.

Process Supervision is a key architectural pattern in Erlang. The language provides robust mechanisms for supervisors, which are special processes designed to monitor other processes (workers). When a worker process crashes, the supervisor can take appropriate actions such as restarting the process, escalating the error to a higher-level supervisor, or ignoring it if deemed appropriate. This hierarchical supervision structure forms supervision trees that are fundamental to building resilient systems.

Isolation between processes is another core tenet. Each Erlang process operates in its own memory space and communicates with others via message passing. This isolation prevents errors in one process from corrupting the state of others, thus localizing the impact of any failure. Isolation also simplifies reasoning about process state and enhances the reliability of concurrent operations.

Pattern Matching is heavily utilized in Erlang, not only to write expressive and concise code but also to handle errors. Functions often specify multiple clauses to match against different patterns, each representing a specific set of inputs. If none of the clauses match, an error is raised, which can be caught and propagated according to the supervision strategy. Pattern matching makes it easier to manage different cases, including error scenarios, without extensive conditionals.

Fault Isolation and Recovery are achieved by designing processes to handle specific tasks and ensuring errors are confined strictly to failing processes. For example, when an error occurs, a process may terminate, and a supervisor will decide whether to restart it, replace it, or escalate the problem. This fault recovery strategy ensures that the overall system remains operational even in the presence of individual process failures.

Error Propagation is consciously designed in Erlang using the principles of linking and monitoring. Processes can link to one another, whereby if one process terminates, linked processes receive an exit signal. Alternatively, processes can monitor others, receiving a message if the monitored process terminates. Linking and monitoring provide mechanisms to detect and respond to errors dynamically, allowing for sophisticated error handling constructs.

Illustrating these principles with an example, consider an Erlang process designed to read data from a file and process it:

```
read_file(File) ->
    case file:open(File, [read]) of
        {ok, Device} ->
            process_file(Device);
        {error, Reason} ->
            {error, Reason}
    end.

process_file(Device) ->
    case file:read_line(Device) of
        {ok, Data} ->
            handle_data(Data),
            process_file(Device);
        {eof} ->
            file:close(Device),
            done;
        {error, Reason} ->
            file:close(Device),
            {error, Reason}
    end.

handle_data(Data) ->
    % Process the data ...
    ok.
```

In this example, the function read_file/1 attempts to open a file. If successful, process_file/1 reads and processes each line until the end of the file is reached. Errors at different stages (such as opening the file or reading a line) are propagated using return tuples like {error, Reason}. This simple example illustrates the basic idea of letting functions fail gracefully and propagating errors upward.

This approach scales naturally to more complex scenarios involving supervisors. A supervisor might be defined to restart the read process if it crashes, thereby ensuring the system's continued operation despite transient errors. Such a supervisor may look as follows:

```
-module(file_supervisor).
-behaviour(supervisor).

-export([start_link/0, init/1]).

start_link() ->
    supervisor:start_link({local, ?MODULE}, ?MODULE, []).

init([]) ->
    {ok, {
        {one_for_one, 5, 10},
        [{file_reader, {file_reader, start_link, []}, permanent, brutal_kill, worker, [
            file_reader]}]
    }}.
```

In this supervisor module, the init/1 function defines a one-for-one strategy, meaning if the file_reader process crashes, it will be restarted up to 5 times within 10 seconds. If it exceeds this limit, the supervisor itself might fail, and higher-level supervisors in the supervision tree will take over. This layered recovery strategy is a powerful feature of Erlang's fault tolerance model.

Understanding and applying these core tenets allows developers to design systems that continue to operate robustly under most conditions, gracefully handling errors, and maintaining high availability.

6.2 Exceptions and Error Handling Mechanisms

Handling exceptions and errors is a critical component of robust software design, particularly within fault-tolerant systems. In this section, we will delve into Erlang's mechanisms for dealing with unexpected conditions, the syntax used, and best practices to effectively handle exceptions.

In Erlang, exceptions can be classified into three primary types: errors, throws, and exits. Each type serves a different purpose and is handled differently within the context of error handling and recovery strategies.

Errors: Errors represent unexpected conditions that typically terminate a process. They occur due to exceptional situations such as function calls with inappropriate arguments or syntax errors. The common types of errors include badmatch, function_clause, case_clause, if_clause, and undef. An example is shown below:

```
% An example causing a badmatch error
example(A) ->
  B = 2,
  A = B.
```

When example/1 is called with an argument other than 2, a badmatch error will be triggered.

Throws: Throws are used for non-local returns in Erlang, often facilitated by the throw/1 function. Throws provide a mechanism to exit from deeply nested constructs without error reporting. They are generally targeted towards specific catch constructs, and unlike errors, they are designed for recoverable situations:

```
% Using throw for non-local returns
safe_divide(A, B) ->
```

```
if
  B == 0 -> throw({error, divide_by_zero});
  true -> A / B
end.
```

Here, safe_divide/2 uses throw/1 to signal an invalid division operation without causing an error.

Exits: Exits are initiated by the exit/1 function and are mostly used to handle process termination gracefully. They play a key role in process links and monitor mechanisms within Erlang's concurrency model. An exit signal can either kill or be trapped by a process. The following example demonstrates a simple process exit:

```
% Initiate a process exit
terminate_process(Pid) ->
  exit(Pid, kill).
```

When invoking terminate_process/1, the process identified by Pid receives the kill exit signal.

Catching and handling exceptions: Erlang provides the try..catch construct to handle exceptions locally within a function. This construct can catch all forms of exceptions and handle them appropriately. The syntax is flexible and allows the capture of specific exception classes.

```
% A try-catch example
safe_operation(A, B) ->
  try
    Result = A div B,
    {ok, Result}
  catch
    error:badarith -> {error, invalid_division}
  end.
```

In the above example, an invalid division operation is caught and returned as a tagged tuple {error, invalid_division}.

Exception patterns: The try..catch block can be extended with different patterns to discriminate between exception types. The patterns include throw/1, exit/1, and error/1. Here's an example addressing the different exception types:

```
% Handling different exception types
classify_exception(Expr) ->
  try
    eval(Expr)
  catch
    throw:Reason -> {caught_throw, Reason};
    error:Reason -> {caught_error, Reason};
    exit:Reason -> {caught_exit, Reason}
  end.
```

The function classify_exception/1 attempts to evaluate Expr and returns a tuple indicating the type of exception caught.

Best practices:

- **Avoid Overusing Exceptions**: Exceptions should be for truly exceptional situations. Regular control flows should not rely on exceptions.
- **Use Guard Clauses**: Where possible, use guard clauses to handle predictable conditions directly.
- **Provide Clear Exception Messages**: When raising exceptions, ensure the reasons are informative to facilitate debugging.
- **Recovery Strategy**: Implement appropriate recovery strategies and ensure fallback mechanisms are in place.
- **Logging**: Ensure all exceptions are logged using Erlang's built-in logging mechanisms for post-mortem analysis.

The robust mechanisms provided by Erlang for handling exceptions allow developers to build resilient systems capable of recovering gracefully from unexpected conditions.

6.3 Process Supervision

Process supervision is a fundamental concept in Erlang which ensures system stability by monitoring processes and automatically taking predefined actions when failures occur. In Erlang, supervisors are specialized processes designed to supervise other processes, referred to as workers. The core idea is based on the "let it crash" philosophy, where processes are allowed to fail, and supervisors ensure their recovery.

The centerpiece of process supervision is the supervisor behavior provided by the standard Erlang/OTP framework. Supervisors are designed to manage and restart worker processes upon failure, ensuring high availability and reliability of the system. To utilize process supervision effectively, several key components and concepts must be understood.

supervisor processes are defined by implementing the supervisor behavior module. Below is a typical implementation pattern for an Erlang supervisor:

```
-module(my_supervisor).
-behavior(supervisor).

%% Supervisor Initialization
-export([start_link/0, init/1]).

%% API
start_link() ->
    supervisor:start_link({local, ?MODULE}, ?MODULE, []).

%% Supervisor Callback
init([]) ->
    %% Define worker specifications
    ChildSpecs = [
        {worker1, {worker1, start_link, []}, permanent, 5000, worker, [worker1]}
    ],
    %% Define supervision strategy
    {ok, {{one_for_one, 5, 10}, ChildSpecs}}.
```

A supervisor behavior module must implement the functions defined by the supervisor behavior, typically start_link/0 and init/1. The start_link/0 function is the entry point for starting the supervisor, linking its process to the calling process. The init/1 function defines the child process specifications and the supervision strategy.

Child Specifications

Child specifications detail how child processes are to be managed and restarted. The ChildSpecs list contains tuples specifying each supervised child. Each tuple typically includes:

- ChildName - A unique identifier for the child.
- StartFunction - A tuple specifying the module, function, and arguments for starting the child process.
- Restart - Defines the restart strategy for this particular process (permanent, transient, or temporary).
- Shutdown - Specifies how to shut down the child process (brutal_kill or a time interval).
- Type - Indicates whether the child is a worker or a supervisor (worker or supervisor).
- Modules - Lists the modules implemented by the child process.

In the given example, worker1 is a child specification indicating a permanent worker process job, which will be restarted by the supervisor indefinitely upon failure.

Supervision Strategies

Supervision strategies dictate how supervisors manage multiple child processes, directing their restart behavior when one or more processes fail. Erlang supports several supervision strategies:

- **one_for_one**: If a child process terminates, only that process gets restarted. This is the simplest and most commonly used strategy.
- **one_for_all**: If a child process terminates, all other child processes are terminated and then all processes, including the terminated one, are restarted.
- **rest_for_one**: If a child process terminates, the rest of the child processes, started after the terminated process, are also terminated, then all these processes are restarted.
- **simple_one_for_one**: Used for dynamically managed children. Only one child specification is used, and all children are based on this specification.

An example of specifying the one_for_one strategy in a supervisor's init/1 function is:

```
init([]) ->
    ChildSpecs = [
        {worker1, {worker1, start_link, []}, permanent, 5000, worker, [worker1]},
        {worker2, {worker2, start_link, []}, transient, 3000, worker, [worker2]}
    ],
    {ok, {{one_for_one, 5, 10}, ChildSpecs}}.
```

In the example, worker1 and worker2 have different restart conditions. The supervisor will only restart the specific child process that fails.

Starting and Linking a Supervisor

Starting a supervisor involves creating and linking it to the parent process. This can be achieved using the start_link function:

```
1> my_supervisor:start_link().
{ok, <0.123.0>}
```

The supervisor process is now running, supervising the specified worker processes. If any worker fails, the supervisor will follow the defined strategy to manage and restart the process.

Monitoring the behavior of supervisors and workers is critical in a production environment.

Effective logging and real-time monitoring can help in diagnosing and responding to unforeseen issues. Supervisor trees are extended structures enabling nested supervision, enhancing fault tolerance and system reliability.

Process supervision in Erlang is a robust mechanism that ensures the resilience of distributed systems. By correctly defining and implementing supervisors, developers can build fault-tolerant applications capable of handling process failures gracefully.

6.4 Using Supervision Trees

In Erlang, supervision trees are a critical construct used to ensure fault tolerance and reliable system behavior. A supervision tree is essentially a hierarchical arrangement where supervisor processes oversee worker processes. The main goal is to handle failure in an isolated and manageable way, adhering to the "let it crash" philosophy. In this section, we delve deeper into the structure, configuration, and operation of supervision trees, providing detailed explanations and practical examples.

At the core of supervision trees are supervisors and workers. Supervisors are special processes designed to manage the lifecycle of their child processes, which can be other supervisors or worker processes. The supervisor's primary task is to restart child processes if they fail, ensuring the system remains operational as much as possible. Erlang provides a standard module named supervisor to facilitate this functionality.

A supervisor can be configured using a specification known as the supervisor behavior. The configuration includes the supervision strategy, restart policy, and child process specifications.

```
-module(my_supervisor).
-behaviour(supervisor).

%% API
-export([start_link/0]).
%% Supervisor callbacks
-export([init/1]).

start_link() ->
    supervisor:start_link({local, ?MODULE}, ?MODULE, []).

init([]) ->
    {ok, {{one_for_one, 5, 10},
          [{worker_1, {worker1, start_link, []}, permanent, brutal_kill, worker, [
               worker1]},
```

```
{worker_2, {worker2, start_link, []}, permanent, brutal_kill, worker, [
        worker2]}
]}}.
```

In the above example, we define a simple supervisor module named my_supervisor. The init/1 callback returns a tuple specifying the supervision strategy and a list of child process specifications.

Strategies and Policies

The supervisor behavior supports several supervision strategies and policies:

- one_for_one: If a child process terminates, only that process is restarted.
- one_for_all: If a child process terminates, all other child processes are terminated, and then all are restarted.
- rest_for_one: If a child process terminates, the subsequent child processes (those that were started after the terminated process) are terminated and restarted.
- simple_one_for_one: A simplified variant of one_for_one for dynamically added children with the same configuration.

These strategies allow developers to design systems with various levels of fault isolation and recovery granularity.

Additionally, each child specification includes the following elements:

- Child's ID: Unique identifier for the child process.
- Start function: A tuple describing the module, function, and arguments to start the child.
- Restart policy: Determines if and how the child process should be restarted (e.g., permanent, transient, temporary).
- Shutdown strategy: Describes how the child process should be terminated (e.g., brutal_kill, integer timeout).
- Child type: Specifies whether the child is a worker or a supervisor.
- Modules: A list of modules implemented by the child process.

Practical Example

To illustrate, consider a simple application where we monitor and restart worker processes.

```
%% Worker module implementation
-module(worker1).
-export([start_link/0, init/1]).

start_link() ->
    gen_server:start_link({local, ?MODULE}, ?MODULE, [], []).

init([]) ->
    %% Initialize worker state here
    {ok, #state{}}.

%% Supervisor module implementation
-module(my_supervisor).
-behaviour(supervisor).

-export([start_link/0]).
-export([init/1]).

start_link() ->
    supervisor:start_link({local, ?MODULE}, ?MODULE, []).

init([]) ->
    {ok, {{one_for_one, 5, 10},
          [{worker_1, {worker1, start_link, []}, permanent, brutal_kill, worker, [
              worker1]}]}}.
```

Here, worker1 is designed as a simple worker module. The my_supervisor module ensures that any failure in worker1 will result in the worker being restarted in isolation, adhering to the one_for_one strategy.

Understanding Restart Intensities

An essential aspect of the supervision strategy is managing restart intensities. The parameters 5 and 10 in the supervisor specification represent the maximum restart intensity: the supervisor will tolerate up to 5 restarts within a 10-second window. If this threshold is exceeded, the supervisor itself terminates, propagating the failure up the supervision tree.

Employing appropriate restart intensities is critical to avoid excessive, futile restarts that could lead to cascading failures or resource exhaustion.

Supervision Tree Configuration

Configuring supervision trees effectively requires careful planning and consideration of fault domains within the application. By grouping related processes under appropriate supervision strategies, it is possible to achieve a robust and maintainable system architecture. A layered approach often works best, where top-level supervisors handle critical failures and lower-level supervisors focus on specific functional areas.

Consider a more complex supervision structure:

```
-module(top_supervisor).
-behaviour(supervisor).

-export([start_link/0]).
-export([init/1]).

start_link() ->
    supervisor:start_link({local, ?MODULE}, ?MODULE, []).

init([]) ->
    {ok, {{one_for_all, 3, 60},
          [{supervisor_1, {sub_supervisor_1, start_link, []}, permanent, brutal_kill,
                supervisor, [sub_supervisor_1]},
           {supervisor_2, {sub_supervisor_2, start_link, []}, permanent, brutal_kill,
                supervisor, [sub_supervisor_2]}]}}.
```

In this structure, top_supervisor oversees two sub-supervisors, each managing its respective group of workers. The one_for_all strategy ensures tight coupling: any failure in a sub-supervisor prompts a restart of all child supervisors and their respective workers, maintaining holistic integrity at this level.

Sub-supervisors might be defined as follows:

```
%% Sub-supervisor 1
-module(sub_supervisor_1).
-behaviour(supervisor).

-export([start_link/0]).
-export([init/1]).

start_link() ->
    supervisor:start_link({local, ?MODULE}, ?MODULE, []).

init([]) ->
    {ok, {{one_for_one, 5, 10},
          [{worker_1, {worker1, start_link, []}, permanent, brutal_kill, worker, [
                worker1]},
           {worker_2, {worker2, start_link, []}, permanent, brutal_kill, worker, [
                worker2]}]}}.

%% Sub-supervisor 2
-module(sub_supervisor_2).
-behaviour(supervisor).

-export([start_link/0]).
-export([init/1]).

start_link() ->
    supervisor:start_link({local, ?MODULE}, ?MODULE, []).

init([]) ->
    {ok, {{rest_for_one, 5, 10},
          [{worker_3, {worker3, start_link, []}, permanent, brutal_kill, worker, [
```

```
        worker3]},
    {worker_4, {worker4, start_link, []}, permanent, brutal_kill, worker, [
        worker4]}]}}.
```

Through this multi-layered approach, sub_supervisor_1 follows a one_for_one strategy, isolating failures to individual workers, while sub_supervisor_2 employs the rest_for_one strategy, providing a graduated restart mechanism.

Ultimately, the hierarchical design of supervision trees in Erlang enables nuanced and resilient error handling. Properly configured supervision trees ensure that any fault can be confined and rectified within a well-defined scope, minimizing the impact on the overall system.

6.5 Creating and Managing Workers

In Erlang, the efficient creation and management of worker processes are crucial elements for building reliable and scalable systems. Worker processes perform the core functions of the application, and their management is essential to ensure fault tolerance and efficient resource utilization. This section explores various strategies and practices for creating and managing workers in an Erlang-based system.

Worker Processes

Erlang uses lightweight processes to achieve concurrency and parallelism. A worker process is a dedicated Erlang process responsible for executing a specific task or a set of related tasks. These processes operate asynchronously and communicate via message passing, aligning with Erlang's concurrency model.

spawn/1 and spawn/3 are primary functions used to create processes in Erlang. The spawn/1 function takes a function as an argument, while the spawn/3 function takes a module name, function name, and a list of arguments. Here's an example of how to spawn a simple worker process:

```
-module(worker_demo).
-export([start/0, worker/1]).

start() ->
    spawn(worker_demo, worker, ["worker_1"]).

worker(Name) ->
    io:format("Worker ~p started~n", [Name]),
    loop(Name).
```

```
loop(Name) ->
    receive
        {message, Msg} ->
            io:format("Worker ~p received message: ~p~n", [Name, Msg]),
            loop(Name);
        stop ->
            io:format("Worker ~p stopping~n", [Name]);
        _ ->
            loop(Name)
    end.
```

The start/0 function spawns a worker process executing the worker/1 function. The worker enters a receive loop, waiting for messages. This structure exemplifies the creation and basic operation of a worker process.

Supervising Workers

Supervisors are special processes in Erlang that monitor and manage worker processes. Their role is to ensure that worker processes are restarted when they fail, enhancing fault tolerance. Supervisors follow predefined strategies to determine the conditions under which a worker should be restarted.

A simple supervisor example can be constructed using the supervisor behavior:

```
-module(simple_supervisor).
-behaviour(supervisor).

-export([start_link/0, init/1]).

start_link() ->
    supervisor:start_link({local, ?MODULE}, ?MODULE, []).

init([]) ->
    ProcName = worker_demo,
    RestartStrategy = {one_for_one, 5, 10},
    ChildSpec = {
        ProcName,
        {worker_demo, start, []},
        permanent,
        5000,
        worker,
        [worker_demo]
    },
    {ok, {RestartStrategy, [ChildSpec]}}.
```

In this example, the simple_supervisor module defines a supervisor's child specification. The child specification includes the worker module and the startup function. The one_for_one restart strategy indicates that if a worker process terminates, only that specific process is restarted.

Dynamic Worker Management

A system often requires the dynamic creation and termination of worker processes based on runtime conditions. This can be achieved by introducing a worker pool or similar dynamic management mechanism.

To demonstrate dynamic worker management, consider the following example where a supervisor dynamically spawns and terminates worker processes based on the workload:

```
-module(dynamic_worker_manager).
-behaviour(supervisor).

-export([start_link/0, init/1, start_worker/0, stop_worker/1]).

start_link() ->
    supervisor:start_link({local, ?MODULE}, ?MODULE, []).

init([]) ->
    {ok, {{simple_one_for_one, 5, 10}, []}}.

start_worker() ->
    supervisor:start_child(?MODULE, []).

stop_worker(Pid) ->
    supervisor:terminate_child(?MODULE, Pid).
```

Here, the supervisor uses the simple_one_for_one strategy, meaning it can manage an arbitrary number of identical worker processes. Functions start_worker/0 and stop_worker/1 are used to dynamically add and remove workers.

Worker Balancing

Efficient balancing of the workload across multiple worker processes ensures optimal performance and resource utilization. Generic workers or worker pools can be utilized to distribute tasks effectively.

A common approach in Erlang for managing worker pools involves the poolboy library, which provides a simple interface to handle worker pools. Below is a configuration for poolboy:

```
{poolboy, [
    {name, {local, my_worker_pool}},
    {worker_module, worker_demo},
    {size, 10},
    {max_overflow, 5}
]}
```

In this configuration, poolboy manages a pool named my_worker_pool with an initial size of 10 workers and a maximum overflow of 5 additional workers.

Monitoring and Logging

Effective management of workers necessitates robust monitoring and logging to track their health and activity. Erlang's built-in tools, such as observer, error_logger, and recon, provide extensive capabilities for process monitoring and real-time analysis.

For instance, to monitor a worker's status, you might use the following:

```
observer:start().
```

```
# This initiates the Observer GUI, enabling detailed monitoring of processes and their state.
```

By implementing these strategies and leveraging Erlang's powerful features, systems can achieve a high degree of fault tolerance and efficiency in worker process management. This approach aligns with Erlang's philosophy of robust error handling and process supervision, ensuring resilient system design.

6.6 Fault Tolerance Strategies

Fault tolerance in Erlang is fundamental to the reliability and robustness of systems developed using this language. The design principles embedded within Erlang emphasize the importance of creating applications that can continue to operate even when parts of the system fail. This section delves into the specific strategies employed to achieve fault-tolerant systems.

Central to Erlang's fault tolerance approach is the "let it crash" philosophy, which contrasts with traditional defensive programming techniques. Instead of attempting to preemptively handle every possible error within a process, Erlang encourages processes to fail and rely on a supervisory structure to manage such failures. This perspective not only simplifies code but also leverages Erlang's robust supervision and monitoring mechanisms.

Supervision Trees

Supervision trees are hierarchical structures where supervisors manage worker processes and are themselves potentially supervised by higher-level supervisors. Each supervisor is responsible for starting, stopping, and monitoring its child processes as dictated by its supervision strategy. Supervision trees are crucial as they define how a system recovers from failures and thus play a pivotal role in fault tolerance.

A simple configuration of a supervisor is shown below:

```
-module(simple_sup).
-behaviour(supervisor).

%% API
-export([start_link/0]).

%% Supervisor callbacks
-export([init/1]).

start_link() ->
    supervisor:start_link({local, ?MODULE}, ?MODULE, []).

init([]) ->
    {ok, {{one_for_one, 5, 10},
          [{worker1, {worker1, start_link, []}, permanent, 5000, worker, [worker1]},
           {worker2, {worker2, start_link, []}, permanent, 5000, worker, [worker2]}]}}.
```

In this example, the simple_sup module starts a supervisor using the one_for_one strategy. This strategy dictates that if one child process terminates, only that process is restarted. Other strategies include one_for_all, where if one child process terminates, all other child processes are terminated and restarted, and rest_for_one, where if one child process terminates, the subsequent child processes are terminated and restarted.

Redundancy and Load Balancing

Redundancy is a core component of fault tolerance in any distributed system, and Erlang systems leverage redundancy to minimize the impact of process failures. By creating multiple instances of critical processes or applications, the system can switch to a backup instance if the primary instance fails. Load balancing is used in conjunction to distribute tasks evenly across these redundant processes, ensuring optimal usage of resources and quick recovery from failures.

```
%% Example module for load balancing
-module(load_balancer).
-behaviour(gen_server).

%% API
-export([start_link/0, send_request/1]).

%% gen_server callbacks
-export([init/1, handle_call/3, handle_cast/2, handle_info/2, terminate/2,
    code_change/3]).

start_link() ->
    gen_server:start_link({local, load_balancer}, ?MODULE, [], []).

init([]) ->
    %% Initialize state, e.g., list of worker pids
    {ok, {active_workers, []}}.
```

```
send_request(Request) ->
    gen_server:call(load_balancer, {request, Request}).

handle_call({request, Request}, _From, State) ->
    %% Logic to forward request to one of the active workers
    %% Example only: not a complete implementation
    Worker = lists:nth(1, State#state.active_workers), %% Select the first worker
    gen_server:cast(Worker, {work, Request}),
    {reply, ok, State}.
```

In the above example, the load_balancer module could distribute requests to available workers, implementing a basic load balancing strategy.

Failover Mechanisms

Failover mechanisms ensure that if a node or critical process fails, another node or process can assume its responsibilities. Erlang utilizes various strategies for failover, ranging from simple retries to more complex strategies involving distributed supervision and node monitoring.

One such failover mechanism can be implemented using the global module, which helps in registering and resolving globally unique names across a distributed Erlang system. This assists in maintaining a coherent state system-wide and enables seamless failover by redirecting to available resources.

```
%% Example of using global module for failover
-module(failover_example).

%% API
-export([start_link/0, register_global/1, resolve_global/0]).

start_link() ->
    spawn(fun() -> loop() end).

register_global(Name) ->
    global:register_name(Name, self()).

resolve_global(Name) ->
    case global:whereis_name(Name) of
        undefined -> {error, not_found};
        Pid -> {ok, Pid}
    end.

loop() ->
    receive
        {work, Data} ->
            %% Perform work
            loop()
    end.
```

In the failover_example module, processes register themselves using a globally unique name. Another process can resolve this name to obtain the process identifier (PID) and communicate with it. If the process fails, a different process can register the same name, ensuring continuity.

Health Checks and Monitoring

Continuous monitoring of system health is integral to fault tolerance. Erlang provides various means for health checks, including monitoring nodes and processes. By using tools like erlang:monitor/2 and erlang:link/1, systems can detect failures promptly and take corrective actions.

Furthermore, logging mechanisms integrated with monitoring tools like observer provide real-time insights into system performance, aiding in preemptive failure detection and mitigation.

```
%% Example of process monitoring
-module(monitor_example).
-export([start_link/1, monitor_process/1]).

start_link(Process) ->
    spawn(fun() -> monitor_process(Process) end).

monitor_process(Process) ->
    Ref = erlang:monitor(process, Process),
    receive
        {'DOWN', Ref, process, _Pid, _Reason} ->
            %% Handle process termination
            io:format("Process ~p down: ~p~n", [Process, _Reason])
    end.
```

In this example, the monitor_example module monitors the given process and reacts when it detects the process has terminated.

Fault tolerance strategies in Erlang revolve around building robust and self-healing systems. Supervisory structures, redundancy, failover mechanisms, load balancing, and continuous monitoring collectively contribute towards achieving highly fault-tolerant applications capable of sustaining high availability and reliability even in the face of failures. This section illustrates strategies and practices embedded within the Erlang ecosystem that foster the development of resilient systems.

6.7 Logging and Monitoring

Logging and monitoring are critical components in maintaining robust and fault-tolerant Erlang systems. By implementing effective logging and monitoring strategies, developers gain visibility into the application's runtime behavior, which aids in diagnosing issues, understanding system performance, and ensuring smooth operations. Erlang provides several tools and methodologies to facilitate comprehensive logging and monitoring.

Logging with error_logger

Erlang's error_logger module is a fundamental component for logging error messages and system events. The error_logger supports different types of messages such as error, info, and debug messages. Below is a typical use case illustrating how to incorporate error_logger in an application:

```
-module(my_logger).
-export([log_error/1, log_info/1, log_debug/1]).

log_error(Message) ->
    error_logger:error_msg("~p~n", [Message]).

log_info(Message) ->
    error_logger:info_msg("~p~n", [Message]).

log_debug(Message) ->
    error_logger:debug_msg("~p~n", [Message]).
```

Messages logged with error_logger are directed to the standard output, and the logging behavior can be customized through configuration parameters such as error_logger_tty_h.

Redirecting Logs to Files

To persist logs for later analysis, redirecting logging output to files is a common practice. This can be achieved by setting up a custom handler that writes logs to a file:

```
-module(file_logger).
-export([start/0, log_error/1, log_info/1, log_debug/1]).

start() ->
    {ok, File} = file:open("error.log", [write, raw]),
    error_logger:tty(false), % Disable default tty logging
    error_logger:add_report_handler({file_handler, File}).

log_error(Message) ->
    error_logger:error_msg("~p~n", [Message]).

log_info(Message) ->
    error_logger:info_msg("~p~n", [Message]).

log_debug(Message) ->
    error_logger:debug_msg("~p~n", [Message]).
```

In this example, logs are redirected to a file named error.log. The file_logger:start/0 function initializes this setup by opening the file in write mode and configuring error_logger to use the custom file handler.

Monitoring with os:cmd/1 **and OS Tools**

Monitoring system performance and resource utilization is vital for identifying potential bottlenecks and ensuring optimal performance. Erlang enables the integration of operating system commands and tools directly within the application using the os:cmd/1 function. For instance, to monitor CPU and memory usage, developers can execute standard OS commands and parse their output:

```
-module(system_monitor).
-export([get_cpu_usage/0, get_memory_usage/0]).

get_cpu_usage() ->
    Output = os:cmd("top -bn1 | grep 'Cpu(s)'"),
    parse_cpu_output(Output).

get_memory_usage() ->
    Output = os:cmd("free -m | grep 'Mem'"),
    parse_memory_output(Output).

parse_cpu_output(Output) ->
    % Parsing logic for CPU usage
    io:format("CPU Usage: ~s~n", [Output]).

parse_memory_output(Output) ->
    % Parsing logic for memory usage
    io:format("Memory Usage: ~s~n", [Output]).
```

In this example, the system_monitor module defines functions to fetch CPU and memory usage data using OS commands and print the output.

Using observer for Real-Time Monitoring

Erlang also offers the observer application, a graphical tool for real-time monitoring of Erlang nodes. The observer provides insights into different aspects of the system, such as process information, memory usage, and message tracing. It can be launched under the following command:

```
observer:start().
```

This function call opens the observer GUI, allowing users to explore various metrics and visualize system behavior interactively.

Custom Supervisors for Health Checks

Implementing custom supervisors and periodic health checks ensure that critical system components remain functional. Custom health check routines can be incorporated within supervisors to monitor and act upon the state of other processes:

```
-module(health_supervisor).
-behaviour(supervisor).
-export([start_link/0, init/1]).
-export([health_check/0]).

start_link() ->
```

```
    supervisor:start_link({local, ?MODULE}, ?MODULE, []).

init([]) ->
    {ok, {{one_for_one, 5, 10},
          [{worker, periodic_health_check, {worker, periodic_health_check, []},
                permanent, 5000, worker}]}}.

health_check() ->
    %% Perform health check logic
    case is_system_healthy() of
        true -> ok;
        false -> handle_unhealthy_system()
    end.

is_system_healthy() ->
    %% Determine system health status
    true.

handle_unhealthy_system() ->
    %% Actions to handle an unhealthy system state
    error_logger:error_msg("System state is unhealthy!").
```

Here, we define a health_supervisor which periodically performs health checks using the health_check/0 function. The logic for determining system health can be customized within the is_system_healthy/0 function, and appropriate actions are taken when the system is found to be in an unhealthy state.

Effective logging and monitoring are imperative for maintaining system reliability and ensuring quick resolution of issues. By leveraging Erlang's native tools and integrating with OS capabilities, developers can create comprehensive monitoring solutions that bolster fault tolerance and system robustness.

6.8 Case Studies of Fault Tolerance in Erlang Systems

Erlang's fault-tolerance capabilities make it a suitable choice for building robust systems. To effectively illustrate the practical application of the principles discussed in this chapter, we will examine several real-world case studies where Erlang's fault tolerance has been instrumental to success. These case studies highlight different facets of fault tolerance, from process supervision to handling massive concurrency and ensuring high availability.

Case Study 1: Telecom Switching Systems

Erlang was originally developed for use in telecom systems by Ericsson, providing a foundational case study demonstrating its robust error-handling capabilities. Telecom systems require near-zero downtime given their critical role.

```
-module(switch).
-behaviour(gen_server).
-export([start_link/0, init/1, handle_call/3, handle_cast/2, terminate/2, code_change
    /3]).

start_link() ->
    gen_server:start_link({local, ?MODULE}, ?MODULE, [], []).

init([]) ->
    {ok, []}.

handle_call(Call, _From, State) ->
    {reply, ok, State}.

handle_cast(Msg, State) ->
    {noreply, State}.

terminate(_Reason, _State) ->
    ok.

code_change(_OldVsn, State, _Extra) ->
    {ok, State}.
```

This process handles calls and messages in a fault-tolerant manner inherently provided by the gen_server behavior. Restart strategies and supervision are crucial here, ensuring that failed components do not propagate errors across the system. Telecom systems employ hierarchical supervision trees, where each node in the tree supervises its children processes.

```
-module(switch_supervisor).
-behaviour(supervisor).
-export([start_link/0, init/1]).

start_link() ->
    supervisor:start_link({local, ?MODULE}, ?MODULE, []).

init([]) ->
    {ok, {{one_for_one, 5, 10},
          [{switch_worker, {switch, start_link, []},
           permanent, brutal_kill, worker, [switch]}]}}.
```

The one_for_one strategy indicates that if a worker process terminates, only that process will be restarted. This localized fault handling ensures minimal service disruption.

Case Study 2: Instant Messaging Systems

Erlang forms the backbone of many instant messaging systems due to its ability to manage massive concurrency effectively. Systems like WhatsApp leverage Erlang's fault tolerance to handle millions of concurrent users.

```
-module(user_session).
-behaviour(gen_server).
-export([start_link/1, init/1, handle_call/3, handle_cast/2, terminate/2, code_change
    /3]).

start_link(UserID) ->
    gen_server:start_link({local, {user_session, UserID}}, ?MODULE, [UserID], []).

init([UserID]) ->
    {ok, #user_session{user_id = UserID, message_queue = queue:new()}}.

handle_call({send_message, Message}, _From, State) ->
    State1 = enqueue_message(State, Message),
    {reply, ok, State1}.

handle_cast({receive_message, Message}, State) ->
    State1 = handle_incoming_message(State, Message),
    {noreply, State1}.

terminate(_Reason, _State) ->
    ok.

code_change(_OldVsn, State, _Extra) ->
    {ok, State}.
```

The user_session module handles user-specific messages, ensuring each session operates independently. This modular design allows the system to restart failed sessions without impacting overall service.

Case Study 3: E-Commerce Platforms

E-commerce platforms manage diverse transactions, necessitating high fault tolerance to maintain trust and reliability. Erlang enables these platforms to handle variable loads efficiently. Processes are supervised to manage diverse tasks such as order processing and inventory management.

```
-module(order_process).
-behaviour(gen_server).
-export([start_link/1, init/1, handle_call/3, handle_cast/2, terminate/2, code_change
    /3]).

start_link(OrderID) ->
    gen_server:start_link({local, {order_process, OrderID}}, ?MODULE, [OrderID], [])
    .

init([OrderID]) ->
    {ok, #order{order_id = OrderID, status = pending}}.

handle_call({process_order, OrderDetails}, _From, State) ->
    case verify_order(OrderDetails) of
        ok ->
            {reply, {processed, OrderID}, State};
        {error, Reason} ->
            {stop, Reason, {error, Reason}, State}
    end.
```

```
handle_cast({update_status, NewStatus}, State) ->
    State1 = State#order{status = NewStatus},
    {noreply, State1}.

terminate(_Reason, _State) ->
    log_order_failure(_Reason),
    ok.

code_change(_OldVsn, State, _Extra) ->
    {ok, State}.
```

The order_process module captures the steps necessary for processing an order. By incorporating order verification and status updates, the system ensures each order's successful completion strictly adheres to pre-set rules. Supervision, in this instance, governs recovery strategies to ameliorate diverse failure types, such as network errors or payment gateway issues.

The examination of these case studies shows Erlang's proven capacity to maintain high service reliability and availability across several critical domains. Each instance is a testament to the language's built-in fault-tolerance mechanisms, such as lightweight process supervision and the robustness of its concurrent processing model.

Chapter 7

OTP Framework

This chapter introduces the OTP framework, detailing its design principles and core components. It covers GenServer and GenEvent behaviors, supervisors, and applications. The chapter also explains OTP applications and releases, utilizing OTP libraries, and provides insights into building and running OTP applications. Case studies are included to demonstrate practical applications of the OTP framework.

7.1 Introduction to OTP

The Open Telecom Platform (OTP) is an extensive suite of libraries and design principles explicitly engineered for scalable and fault-tolerant software development. Originally designed by Ericsson for telecom systems, OTP has become a cornerstone for building robust systems in various domains, leveraging the inherent capabilities of the Erlang language.

OTP embodies a recursive design philosophy, encapsulating system behaviors and structuring complex systems hierarchically. Central to OTP are its behaviors, supervision trees, and the principles of concurrent and distributed systems design. This section delves into these fundamental concepts, setting the stage for detailed explorations in subsequent chapters.

Behaviors in OTP define a set of callback functions that specify the expected behavior of a module. The two primary behaviors covered in this chapter are gen_server and gen_event. These behaviors abstract the common patterns used in server and event handler processes, respectively, standardizing their implementation.

The gen_server behavior is a generic server that abstracts the common architectural pattern of a server that manages state and handles client requests synchronously or asynchronously. To implement a gen_server, one must define a set of callback functions that adhere to the gen_server behavior's specifications. Consider the following example, which outlines the structure of a simple gen_server module:

```
-module(simple_server).
-behaviour(gen_server).

-export([start_link/0, stop/0]).
-export([init/1, handle_call/3, handle_cast/2, terminate/2]).

start_link() ->
    gen_server:start_link({local, ?MODULE}, ?MODULE, [], []).

stop() ->
    gen_server:call(?MODULE, stop).

init([]) ->
    {ok, #state{}}.

handle_call(stop, _From, State) ->
    {stop, normal, ok, State};
handle_call(_Request, _From, State) ->
    {reply, ok, State}.

handle_cast(_Msg, State) ->
    {noreply, State}.

terminate(_Reason, _State) ->
    ok.
```

In this example, the start_link/0 function initiates the gen_server, and the stop/0 function sends a stop request to the server. The init/1 function initializes the server state. Callback functions such as handle_call/3 and handle_cast/2 manage synchronous calls and asynchronous messages, respectively, maintaining a standardized approach for handling inter-process communications.

The gen_event behavior handles event notifications, allowing multiple handlers to subscribe to events and react to them. The following example illustrates how to define a simple event handler using gen_event:

```
-module(simple_event).
-behaviour(gen_event).

-export([init/1, handle_event/2, handle_info/2, terminate/2]).

init([]) ->
```

```
    {ok, #state{}}.

handle_event(Event, State) ->
    io:format("Received event: ~p~n", [Event]),
    {ok, State}.

handle_info(_Info, State) ->
    {ok, State}.

terminate(_Reason, _State) ->
    ok.
```

This event handler prints the received event to the console. The handle_event/2 function processes the event, and handle_info/2 processes any additional information sent to the event handler. The terminate/2 function handles the termination of the event handler.

Supervision trees are a critical OTP design pattern for building fault-tolerant systems. They organize processes hierarchically, allowing systems to isolate faults and recover gracefully. Supervisors are special processes that monitor worker processes and apply specified restart strategies when failures occur. For instance, a simple supervisor might be defined as follows:

```
-module(simple_sup).
-behaviour(supervisor).

-export([start_link/0, init/1]).

start_link() ->
    supervisor:start_link({local, ?MODULE}, ?MODULE, []).

init([]) ->
    ChildSpecs = [
        {simple_server, {simple_server, start_link, []},
        permanent, 5000, worker, [simple_server]}
    ],
    {ok, {{one_for_one, 1, 5}, ChildSpecs}}.
```

In this example, the simple_sup supervisor starts and monitors the simple_server process using the one_for_one restart strategy, which restarts the child process if it fails. The supervisor specification includes details such as restart frequency and intensity, ensuring controlled fault recovery.

OTP's concurrency and distribution capabilities extend to its application framework for managing large-scale solutions. An application groups related supervised processes under a unified structure, facilitating deployment, upgrading, and maintenance. Key to applications is the .app file, which defines application metadata, dependencies, and entry points. The example below illustrates a minimal .app file for the simple_app application:

```
{application, simple_app,
 [{description, "A simple OTP application"},
  {vsn, "0.1"},
  {modules, [simple_server, simple_event, simple_sup]},
  {registered, [simple_server]},
  {applications, [kernel, stdlib]},
  {mod, {simple_app, []}},
  {env, []}
 ]}.
```

This file describes the application with its version, involved modules, required applications (kernel and stdlib), and the application callback module (simple_app). Such structure empowers seamless integration and consistent management of complex systems.

Understanding these fundamental OTP concepts and components provides a foundation for building resilient and scalable systems, essential in the subsequent chapters' detailed discussions and exemplifications. By adhering to OTP's structured approach, developers can achieve high availability, maintainability, and robustness in their applications. Throughout this book, the progressive elaboration of these concepts will enable deeper insights and practical applications, enhancing your proficiency in mastering the OTP framework with Erlang.

7.2 OTP Design Principles

The Open Telecom Platform (OTP) is a collection of middleware, libraries, and tools designed to help developers create robust, fault-tolerant applications. The design principles of OTP are integral to understanding how to leverage its capabilities effectively. These principles serve as guidelines to ensure that applications are not only resilient but also easy to maintain and scale.

Principle 1: Separation of Concerns

OTP emphasizes the decomposition of a system into manageable components, each with a distinct responsibility. This principle, often known as separation of concerns, allows for better organization and reduced complexity. By isolating different aspects of the application into their own modules or processes, developers can focus on individual functionalities without being overwhelmed by the entire system's complexity. The use of behaviors, such as GenServer and GenEvent, inherently supports this principle by encapsulating specific functionalities within defined callbacks.

Principle 2: Redundancy and Fault-Tolerance

Fault-tolerance is at the heart of OTP's design. Systems are expected to encounter failures, and OTP's structure prepares for such eventualities by allowing for redundancy in design. Supervisor trees, a core aspect of OTP, exemplify this principle. Supervisors monitor and manage worker processes, restarting them when failures occur based on specified strategies. This ensures that the system can continue to function even when individual components fail.

```
% Supervisor Example
-module(my_sup).
-behaviour(supervisor).

init([]) ->
    {ok, {{one_for_one, 5, 10},
          [
            {worker1, {worker1, start_link, []}, permanent, 2000, worker, [worker1]},
            {worker2, {worker2, start_link, []}, permanent, 2000, worker, [worker2]}
          ]
         }
    }.
```

In the above example, the supervisor is configured to manage two workers, worker1 and worker2, each of which will be restarted if they fail.

Principle 3: Concurrency

OTP leverages Erlang's lightweight process model to achieve high levels of concurrency. Each component, whether it be a worker, server, or event handler, can operate independently as an Erlang process. This concurrent execution allows OTP applications to efficiently utilize system resources, particularly on multi-core architectures. Processes in Erlang are isolated and communicate via message passing, which enhances the robustness and reliability of the system, as failures in one process do not directly affect others.

```
% Example of Concurrency with Processes
-module(concurrent_example).
-export([start/0, worker/1]).

start() ->
    spawn(concurrent_example, worker, [10]),
    spawn(concurrent_example, worker, [20]).

worker(Times) ->
    lists:foreach(fun(_) -> io:format("Working~n") end, lists:seq(1, Times)).
```

In this example, two worker processes are spawned concurrently, each executing its task independently.

Principle 4: Scalability

Scalability is an intrinsic part of OTP design. OTP applications can easily scale both vertically, by optimizing process distribution across multiple cores or CPUs, and horizontally, by distributing load across multiple nodes in a network. The supervisor hierarchy is designed to be extensible, allowing new processes to be added without disrupting the existing system. Additionally, the use of distributed Erlang facilitates the seamless communication and coordination required for horizontal scaling.

Principle 5: Maintainability

Maintainable code is easier to understand, debug, and extend. OTP's behaviors, such as GenServer, GenEvent, and Supervisor, provide a structured way to implement common patterns, reducing boilerplate code and enhancing readability. The callback mechanisms enforced by these behaviors ensure that the code adheres to defined patterns, making it easier for developers to reason about system behavior.

```
% GenServer Example
-module(my_gen_server).
-behaviour(gen_server).

%% API
-export([start_link/0, call/1, cast/1]).
-export([init/1, handle_call/3, handle_cast/2, handle_info/2, terminate/2,
        code_change/3]).

start_link() ->
    gen_server:start_link({local, ?MODULE}, ?MODULE, [], []).

call(Request) ->
    gen_server:call(?MODULE, Request).

cast(Message) ->
    gen_server:cast(?MODULE, Message).

%% gen_server callbacks
init([]) ->
    {ok, []}.

handle_call(_Request, _From, State) ->
    {reply, ok, State}.

handle_cast(_Message, State) ->
    {noreply, State}.

handle_info(_Info, State) ->
    {noreply, State}.

terminate(_Reason, _State) ->
    ok.

code_change(_OldVsn, State, _Extra) ->
    {ok, State}.
```

This GenServer example contains all necessary callbacks, demonstrating the structured approach that facilitates maintainability.

Principle 6: Observability

Observability refers to the ability to monitor and understand the internal state of an application. OTP provides robust tools such as Observer, sys, and dbg modules to enable developers to inspect and debug running systems. Proper logging and monitoring are critical for diagnosing issues and optimizing performance, ensuring that potential problems can be detected and resolved promptly.

By understanding and applying these design principles, developers can fully exploit the capabilities of OTP to build resilient, scalable, and maintainable applications. Each principle interlocks to create a framework that addresses many common challenges in software development, enhancing both productivity and code quality.

7.3 GenServer and GenEvent Behaviors

GenServer and GenEvent are two cornerstones of the OTP framework, providing essential abstractions for building robust and maintainable Erlang applications. Understanding these behaviors is crucial for leveraging the full power of OTP.

GenServer (short for Generic Server) abstracts the common patterns of a server process. A GenServer simplifies process management, allowing developers to focus on the business logic rather than the boilerplate code. The GenServer API provides a consistent way to handle synchronous and asynchronous communications, process life cycle events, and state management.

```
-module(my_gen_server).
-behaviour(gen_server).

%% API
-export([start_link/0]).

%% gen_server callbacks
-export([init/1, handle_call/3, handle_cast/2, handle_info/2, terminate/2,
      code_change/3]).

start_link() ->
    gen_server:start_link({local, ?MODULE}, ?MODULE, [], []).

init([]) ->
    {ok, #state{data = #{}}}.
```

In this example, the start_link/0 function initializes a new GenServer process. The gen_server:start_link/4 function is utilized to start the server and link it to the current process. The init/1 callback initializes the state, which can be customized as required.

The GenServer behavior also includes other essential callbacks such as handle_call/3, handle_cast/2, and handle_info/2 for synchronous calls, asynchronous casts, and handling other messages, respectively.

```
handle_call({get, Key}, _From, State) ->
    {reply, maps:get(Key, State#state.data), State};
handle_call({set, Key, Value}, _From, State) ->
    NewData = maps:put(Key, Value, State#state.data),
    {reply, ok, State#state{data = NewData}}.
```

In handle_call/3, different types of synchronous requests are managed. For example, to retrieve a value associated with a key or to set a new key-value pair in the state. The state is represented as a map which is updated and returned in the handle_call/3.

Asynchronous messages are handled by the handle_cast/2 callback:

```
handle_cast({put, Key, Value}, State) ->
    NewData = maps:put(Key, Value, State#state.data),
    {noreply, State#state{data = NewData}}.
```

The handle_cast/2 function processes asynchronous requests, modifying the state without providing an immediate reply.

Termination of a GenServer and code changes are managed by terminate/2 and code_change/3 callbacks, respectively:

```
terminate(_Reason, _State) ->
    ok.

code_change(_OldVsn, State, _Extra) ->
    {ok, State}.
```

These callbacks ensure that the server process can be cleanly terminated and adapted to code upgrades even while running.

GenEvent (short for Generic Event) is used for implementing event management. The GenEvent behavior allows for the creation of an event manager which can register handlers that react to a set of events. This pattern is particularly useful in logging, monitoring, and other scenarios requiring decoupled event management.

A typical GenEvent setup involves creating an event manager, adding handlers, and emitting events.

```
start_event_manager() ->
```

```
    gen_event:start_link({local, event_mgr}).

add_handler(Handler, Args) ->
    gen_event:add_handler(event_mgr, Handler, Args).
```

Event handlers are modules implementing the GenEvent behavior, defining callbacks such as handle_event/2, handle_info/2, and terminate/2.

```
-module(my_event_handler).
-behaviour(gen_event).

%% gen_event callbacks
-export([init/1, handle_event/2, handle_info/2, terminate/2]).

init(Args) ->
    {ok, Args}.

handle_event({msg, Message}, State) ->
    io:format("Received message: ~p~n", [Message]),
    {ok, State};
handle_event(_Event, State) ->
    {ok, State}.

handle_info(_Info, State) ->
    {ok, State}.

terminate(_Reason, _State) ->
    ok.
```

Here, the my_event_handler module specifies how the event handler reacts to events. The handle_event/2 function processes incoming events.

To emit events, the gen_event:notify/2 function is used:

```
emit_event(Event) ->
    gen_event:notify(event_mgr, Event).
```

This function sends an event to the event manager, which then dispatches it to all registered handlers.

By leveraging GenServer and GenEvent behaviors, Erlang developers can build scalable and maintainable applications, adhering to the principles of the OTP framework. Understanding these abstractions facilitates the creation of robust systems capable of handling complex requirements with clear separation of concerns.

7.4 Supervisors and Applications

Supervisors are a cornerstone of the OTP framework, residing at the heart of its fault-tolerant design. A supervisor is a process whose primary responsibility is to monitor and manage other processes, termed child processes. When a child process terminates, a supervisor can take predefined actions such as restarting the child or all its children, thereby ensuring system reliability.

Supervisor Behavior

The supervisor behavior is implemented using the supervisor module, which defines a standard interface and functionality for process supervision. Supervisors manage child processes according to a specified strategy. The primary supervisor strategies include:

- one_for_one: Restarts the terminated child process only.
- one_for_all: Restarts all child processes if one terminates.
- rest_for_one: Restarts the terminated child and any subsequent child processes.
- simple_one_for_one: Handles dynamically added children, restarting each individually.

A supervisor is typically defined in a module and initialized with the init/1 callback function which returns a supervision specification, usually structured as a tuple {ok, {SupFlags, [ChildSpec]}}.

```
-module(my_supervisor).
-behaviour(supervisor).

%% API
-export([start_link/0]).
%% Supervisor callbacks
-export([init/1]).

start_link() ->
    supervisor:start_link({local, ?MODULE}, ?MODULE, []).

init([]) ->
    RestartStrategy = one_for_one,
    MaxRestarts = 10,
    MaxTime = 3600,
    SupFlags = {RestartStrategy, MaxRestarts, MaxTime},
    ChildSpecs = [
        %% Define your child processes here
```

```
        {my_worker, {my_worker, start_link, []},
         permanent, 5000, worker, [my_worker]}
    ],
    {ok, {SupFlags, ChildSpecs}}.
```

This example sets up a simple supervisor with a one_for_one strategy.

Defining Applications

In OTP, an application is a component implementing a specific functionality, packaged as a reusable unit. An OTP application typically consists of several modules, optionally including a supervision tree, configuration files, and metadata. Applications are specified using an .app file, which contains key information such as application name, version, and module start points.

Example of an .app file:

```
{application, my_app,
 [{description, "My OTP Application"},
  {vsn, "1.0.0"},
  {modules, [my_worker, my_supervisor]},
  {registered, []},
  {applications, [kernel, stdlib]},
  {mod, {my_app, []}},
  {env, []},
  {start_phases, undefined},
  {maxT, {restart, permanent}},
  {args, []}]}.
```

The mod attribute specifies the callback module that OTP will invoke to start the application's supervision tree.

Start and Stop Callbacks

The callback module for an application must implement the application behavior, specifically the start/2 and stop/1 callbacks. The start/2 function typically initiates the top-level supervisor.

```
-module(my_app).
-behaviour(application).

-export([start/2, stop/1]).

start(_StartType, _StartArgs) ->
    my_supervisor:start_link().

stop(_State) ->
    ok.
```

Integrating with Releases

An essential aspect of OTP applications is their seamless integration into releases, which bundle one or more applications into a deliverable format. Releases ensure that versions are consistent and dependencies are met. They include a .rel file describing the applications involved.

Example of a .rel file:

```
{release, {"my_release", "1"},
  {erts, "10.7"},
  [{kernel, "6.5"},
   {stdlib, "3.12"},
   {my_app, "1.0.0"}]}.
```

Releases are built using tools such as rebar or relx. Once built, a release can be deployed and started using bin scripts, managing the full application lifecycle from startup to shutdown.

Integrating supervisors and applications within the OTP framework thus allows for robust, maintainable, and fault-tolerant design, ensuring systems can recover elegantly from failures and manage processes efficiently. The proper structuring of applications and releases encapsulates modular functionality and supports dynamic system upgrades.

7.5 OTP Applications and Releases

OTP Applications are fundamental components within the OTP framework, comprising a structured way of building, packaging, and deploying Erlang-based systems. Each application is a compilation of modules, libraries, and resources designed to work cohesively to perform specific tasks. Understanding the configuration and implementation of OTP Applications is crucial for leveraging the OTP framework's full power.

Application is a packaging component defined by an application specification, typically written in a file named .app. The specification file contains metadata that includes the application's name, version, modules, registered processes, and various configuration parameters.

Release is a packaging component that includes one or more applications, along with the runtime environment necessary for their execution. Releases are defined with .rel files, detailing the contained applications, their versions, and other runtime requirements.

The following sections delve into creating and configuring OTP applications and releases by outlining their specifications, configurations, and practical implementation details.

```
{application, myapp,
 [{description, "My Application"},
  {vsn, "0.1.0"},
  {modules, [myapp_module1, myapp_module2]},
  {registered, [myapp_server]},
  {applications, [kernel, stdlib, other_application]},
  {mod, {myapp_app, []}},
  {env, [{param1, value1}, {param2, value2}]}
 ]}.
```

A closer inspection of the .app file reveals the following fields:

- description: A brief description of the application.
- vsn: The version of the application.
- modules: A list of modules included in the application.
- registered: The names of registered processes.
- applications: Specifies other OTP applications required.
- mod: Identifies the callback module and its arguments.
- env: Provides a list of key-value pairs for configuration.

start/2 and stop/1 call-back functions are essential, which the mod field references. These functions are defined within the callback module myapp_app.erl as illustrated:

```
-module(myapp_app).
-behaviour(application).

%% Application callbacks
-export([start/2, stop/1]).

start(_Type, _Args) ->
  case myapp_sup:start_link() of
    {ok, Pid} ->
      {ok, Pid};
    {error, Reason} ->
      {error, Reason}
  end.

stop(_State) ->
  ok.
```

In the callback module, start/2 initializes the application by starting the supervisor, which is responsible for managing the application's processes.

Releases are described using .rel files which are processed by release_-handler. Releases define the OTP system configuration, including the versions of applications and their dependencies.

```
{release, {"OTP","R23"},
 [{erts, "11.1.3"},
  {kernel, "7.0"},
  {stdlib, "3.13.2"},
  {myapp, "0.1.0"}
 ]}.
```

The .rel file contains:

- release: The release identifier, including the OTP version.
- applications: The list of applications along with their versions.

With the specifications in place, the project can be built using tools like rebar3 to generate releases. A basic rebar.config example for application myapp is shown below:

```
{erl_opts, [debug_info]}.
{deps, []}.
{applications, [kernel, stdlib, other_application]}.
{relx, [{release, {myapp, "0.1.0"}, [myapp]},
        {dev_mode, true},
        {include_erts, false},
        {extended_start_script, true}
       ]}.
```

Creating a release involves executing the build command:

```
$ rebar3 release
```

When successfully built, the release is found under the _build/default-/rel directory, containing all files necessary to run the application, including a start script.

An example execution of the release startup script might resemble:

```
$ _build/default/rel/myapp/bin/myapp start
```

This comprehensive arrangement ensures that all necessary applications and configurations are encapsulated within the OTP release, readily deployable as a single entity, facilitating smooth updates and maintenance. Detailed understanding and correct implementation of these principles are pivotal for any developer working with the OTP framework.

7.6 Using OTP Libraries

Erlang's Open Telecom Platform (OTP) framework includes a set of libraries specifically designed to aid in building robust, scalable, and maintainable applications. These libraries are integral to the OTP ecosystem, providing tools and modules to address common needs such as error handling, logging, and application configuration. This section delves into the most frequently used OTP libraries and demonstrates how to harness their capabilities in your projects.

Firstly, we explore the logger module, which offers a flexible logging infrastructure. The logger module enables developers to generate log messages across various levels (e.g., debug, info, warning, error) and direct these messages to different handlers, such as console, file, or custom handlers.

To initialize logging in an OTP application, the following setup code is used:

```
logger:add_handlers([logger_std_h, logger_file_h]),

logger:info("Application started successfully"),
logger:debug("Debugging message: ~p", [DebugInfo]),
logger:warn("Warning: ~s", ["A potential issue occurred"]),
logger:error("Error: ~s", ["An error has been encountered"])
```

In this example, the logger:add_handlers/1 function adds standard and file-based handlers, thus activating them for log message processing. Subsequent logging functions such as logger:info/1, logger:debug/2, logger:warn/2, and logger:error/2 generate log messages at the respective levels.

Another essential OTP library is application. This module provides several functions which facilitate application resource management, configuration, and lifecycle control. The application module is central to OTP's application management paradigm. To start and stop an OTP application, use:

```
ok = application:start(my_app),
ok = application:stop(my_app)
```

Additionally, the application:get_env/1 function can be used to fetch environment variables defined in an application's configuration file:

```
case application:get_env(my_app, some_key) of
    {ok, Value} -> io:format("Env variable found:~n Value = ~p", [Value]);
    undefined -> io:format("Env variable not found")
end
```

OTP also includes robust error handling libraries, such as supervisor and supervisor_bridge. These libraries enable fault-tolerant design by monitoring worker processes and restarting them when necessary. A supervisor's child specification, which defines how child processes should be started and managed, appears as follows:

```
ChildSpec = {child_id, {module_name, start_link, [Arg1, Arg2]}, permanent, 5000,
    worker, [module_name]},
{ok, SupPid} = supervisor:start_link(SupModule, [ChildSpec])
```

In this specification, child_id uniquely identifies the child process, start_link refers to the function used to start the child process, and permanent indicates that the child should be restarted indefinitely if it terminates. The restart intensity and shutdown time are also specified, along with the child's type (in this case, a worker).

Another particularly powerful OTP library is gen_server. This module implements the GenServer behavior, encapsulating the generic server functionality. It abstracts common patterns such as synchronous calls, asynchronous casts, state management, and system message processing.

An example of a simple GenServer implementation is shown here:

```
-module(my_gen_server).
-behaviour(gen_server).

-export([start_link/0, init/1, handle_call/3, handle_cast/2, terminate/2]).

start_link() ->
    gen_server:start_link({local, ?MODULE}, ?MODULE, [], []).

init([]) ->
    {ok, #state{}}.

handle_call(Request, _From, State) ->
    {reply, Response, State}.

handle_cast(Msg, State) ->
    {noreply, State}.

terminate(_Reason, _State) ->
    ok.
```

This code defines a GenServer module with initialization, call handling, cast handling, and termination functions. The start_link/0 function starts the server, while the init/1 function initializes its state. The handle_call/3 manages synchronous call messages, and the handle_-cast/2 manages asynchronous cast messages. The terminate/2 function cleans up any necessary state upon termination.

The OTP libraries empower developers to build applications that are modular, reliable, and maintainable. Through judicious use of logger for logging, application for lifecycle management, supervisor for fault tolerance, and gen_server for implementing server behaviors, one can significantly streamline development processes and enhance application robustness and scalability.

7.7 Building and Running OTP Applications

The process of building and running OTP applications involves several critical steps, from defining the application's structure to deploying it in a production environment. This section will delve into defining the application structure, setting up necessary configuration files, compiling the code, and running the application. Understanding this lifecycle is essential for effective management and implementation of robust, scalable Erlang-based systems.

Defining the Application Structure

An OTP application typically comprises multiple components, including modules, processes, and supervisors. The structure is defined in the .app resource file, which contains metadata about the application, such as its name, version, modules, and start function. Here is an example of an app.resource file:

```
{application, myapp,
 [{description, "My First OTP Application"},
  {vsn, "1.0"},
  {modules, [myapp, myapp_sup, myapp_server]},
  {registered, [myapp_server]},
  {applications, [kernel, stdlib]},
  {mod, {myapp_app, []}},
  {env, []}
 ]}.
```

In this file, myapp is the application name, vsn denotes the version, and the modules list includes all Erlang modules that make up the application. The registered list enumerates the names of any processes that should be globally registered. The applications attribute specifies dependencies required before this application can start, and mod points to the module and function that initializes the application.

Setting Up Application Configuration

Configuration plays a significant role in OTP applications. Typically, configuration files are written in Erlang terms and include parameters that configure runtime behavior such as file paths, network ports, and other environment-specific settings. A common practice is to separate configuration values into a sys.config file which can be edited without altering the source code.

Here is an example sys.config file:

```
[{myapp,
  [{parameter1, value1},
   {parameter2, value2}
  ]}
].
```

In this fragment, the myapp tuple contains settings specific to the myapp application. Each parameter can be accessed within the Erlang code using the application:get_env/1 function.

Compiling the Code

Erlang applications are compiled using erlc, the Erlang compiler. OTP provides a build tool called rebar that greatly simplifies the compilation process, especially for larger projects. A typical rebar.config file might look like:

```
{erl_opts, [debug_info]}.
{deps, [{cowboy, ".*", {git, "https://github.com/ninenines/cowboy.git", {tag, "2.6.3"
    }}}]}.
{relx, [{release, {"myapp", "1.0"},
          [myapp, sasl]},
         {dev_mode, true},
         {include_erts, false},
         {extended_start_script, true}
        ]}.
```

This configuration file specifies the dependencies, compiler options, and release details. rebar3 automates fetching dependencies, compiling code, and generating release packages.

To compile the application:

```
$ rebar3 compile
```

The output of this command will look similar to:

```
===> Compiling myapp
===> Compiling src/myapp_server.erl
===> Compiling src/myapp_sup.erl
===> Compiling src/myapp_app.erl
```

Running the Application

Once the application is compiled, it can be run using the Erlang shell or as a standalone release. To start the application in the Erlang shell:

```
$ erl -pa _build/default/lib/myapp/ebin
```

```
1> application:start(myapp).
```

This will output:

```
ok
```

For production environments, it is more common to run the application as a release. A release bundles the application with its dependencies, the Erlang runtime, and a custom start script. Using rebar3, a release is built with:

```
$ rebar3 release
```

The resulting executable can be found in the _build/default/rel/myapp/bin directory. To start the release, execute:

```
$ ./_build/default/rel/myapp/bin/myapp console
```

The console will display:

```
Erlang/OTP 24 [erts-11.2.2] [source] [64-bit] [smp:4:4] [ds:4:4:10] [async-threads:1] [hipe]

Eshell V11.2.2  (abort with ^G)
(myapp@hostname)1>
```

Here, the release is running, and the Erlang shell is accessible. To detach from the console while keeping the application running in the background, use:

```
$ ./_build/default/rel/myapp/bin/myapp start
```

Monitoring the application's runtime behavior can be achieved using observer and SASL tools for logging and tracing. Understanding these processes ensures a smooth transition from development to production in OTP applications.

7.8 Case Studies in OTP

In this section, we delve into practical implementations of the OTP framework by presenting detailed case studies. These examples consolidate concepts introduced in previous sections and illustrate how to deploy OTP for real-world applications.

Case Study 1: Chat Application

One quintessential example for understanding the power of OTP is a chat application. The chat application involves multiple interconnected components, each of which lends itself well to OTP's structured approach.

To begin, we define a GenServer to handle user registration and message distribution. Start by implementing the UserRegistry to manage user sessions.

```
-module(user_registry).
-behaviour(gen_server).

%% API
-export([start_link/0, register_user/1, send_message/2, get_messages/1]).

%% gen_server callbacks
-export([init/1, handle_call/3, handle_cast/2, handle_info/2, terminate/2,
    code_change/3]).

-record(state, {users = #{}}).

start_link() ->
  gen_server:start_link({local, ?MODULE}, ?MODULE, [], []).

register_user(User) ->
  gen_server:call(?MODULE, {register_user, User}).

send_message(User, Msg) ->
  gen_server:cast(?MODULE, {send_message, User, Msg}).

get_messages(User) ->
  gen_server:call(?MODULE, {get_messages, User}).

init([]) ->
  {ok, #state{}}.

handle_call({register_user, User}, _From, State) ->
  {reply, ok, State#state{users = maps:put(User, [], State#state.users)}};

handle_call({get_messages, User}, _From, State) ->
  case maps:find(User, State#state.users) of
    {ok, Messages} -> {reply, {ok, Messages}, State};
    error -> {reply, {error, user_not_found}, State}
  end;

handle_cast({send_message, User, Msg}, State) ->
  UpdatedState = update_user_messages(User, Msg, State),
  {noreply, UpdatedState}.

handle_info(_, State) ->
  {noreply, State}.

terminate(_, _) ->
  ok.

code_change(_, State, _) ->
  {ok, State}.

update_user_messages(User, Msg, State) ->
  Users = State#state.users,
  case maps:find(User, Users) of
    {ok, Messages} ->
      NewUserState = maps:update(User, Messages ++ [Msg], Users),
```

```
        State#state{users = NewUserState};
    error ->
        State
  end.
```

The UserRegistry GenServer initializes with an empty state and handles synchronous call requests for user registration and retrieving messages. Asynchronous cast handles message sending.

To build on this, consider incorporating a supervisor to manage the lifecycle of the UserRegistry.

```
-module(chat_supervisor).
-behaviour(supervisor).

%% API
-export([start_link/0]).

%% supervisor callbacks
-export([init/1]).

start_link() ->
  supervisor:start_link({local, ?MODULE}, ?MODULE, []).

init([]) ->
  {ok, {{one_for_one, 5, 10},
        [{user_registry, {user_registry, start_link, []},
        permanent, 5000, worker, [user_registry]}]}}.
```

Here, a simple one_for_one supervision strategy is configured to restart the user_registry process if it fails.

Case Study 2: Distributed Key-Value Store

A more complex implementation leverages OTP to create a distributed key-value store. Begin with the module definitions, ensuring each node in the cluster can handle key-value operations and replication.

```
-module(distributed_kv).
-behaviour(gen_server).

%% API
-export([start_link/0, insert/2, lookup/1, delete/1]).

%% gen_server callbacks
-export([init/1, handle_call/3, handle_cast/2, handle_info/2, terminate/2,
      code_change/3]).

-record(state, {data = #{}}).

start_link() ->
  gen_server:start_link({local, ?MODULE}, ?MODULE, [], []).

insert(Key, Value) ->
  gen_server:call(?MODULE, {insert, Key, Value}).

lookup(Key) ->
```

```
  gen_server:call(?MODULE, {lookup, Key}).

delete(Key) ->
  gen_server:call(?MODULE, {delete, Key}).

init([]) ->
  {ok, #state{}}.

handle_call({insert, Key, Value}, _From, State) ->
  {reply, ok, State#state{data = maps:put(Key, Value, State#state.data)}};

handle_call({lookup, Key}, _From, State) ->
  case maps:find(Key, State#state.data) of
    {ok, Value} -> {reply, {ok, Value}, State};
    error -> {reply, {error, key_not_found}, State}
  end;

handle_call({delete, Key}, _From, State) ->
  {reply, ok, State#state{data = maps:remove(Key, State#state.data)}}.

handle_cast(_, State) ->
  {noreply, State}.

handle_info(_, State) ->
  {noreply, State}.

terminate(_, _) ->
  ok.

code_change(_, State, _) ->
  {ok, State}.
```

This server maintains key-value pairs using an Erlang map and provides basic CRUD operations. To add replication, integrate a secondary GenServer to act as a replica and propagate changes across the cluster.

```
-module(replica_kv).
-behaviour(gen_server).

%% API
-export([start_link/0, replicate_insert/3, replicate_delete/2]).

%% gen_server callbacks
-export([init/1, handle_call/3, handle_cast/2, handle_info/2, terminate/2,
      code_change/3]).

-record(state, {replicas = []}).

start_link(Replicas) ->
  gen_server:start_link({local, ?MODULE}, ?MODULE, [Replicas], []).

replicate_insert(Replica, Key, Value) ->
  gen_server:cast(Replica, {replicate_insert, Key, Value}).

replicate_delete(Replica, Key) ->
  gen_server:cast(Replica, {replicate_delete, Key}).

init([Replicas]) ->
  {ok, #state{replicas = Replicas}}.
```

```
handle_cast({replicate_insert, Key, Value}, State) ->
  lists:foreach(fun(Replica) -> distributed_kv:insert(Key, Value) end, State#state.
       replicas),
  {noreply, State}.

handle_cast({replicate_delete, Key}, State) ->
  lists:foreach(fun(Replica) -> distributed_kv:delete(Key) end, State#state.replicas),
  {noreply, State}.

handle_call(_, _From, State) ->
  {reply, ok, State}.

handle_info(_, State) ->
  {noreply, State}.

terminate(_, _) ->
  ok.

code_change(_, State, _) ->
  {ok, State}.
```

By retrieving this setup, extending it to a clustered environment is straightforward. Nodes can broadcast changes to maintain consistent state throughout the distributed store, exemplifying OTP's robustness in managing state and resilience.

Case Study 3: Web Server

In this final case study, consider a simplistic web server that benefits from OTP's supervision and reliability. Utilize the cowboy HTTP server and combine it with GenServer for handling requests.

First, define a basic request handler:

```
-module(simple_handler).
-behaviour(cowboy_http_handler).

-export([init/3, handle/2, terminate/3]).

init(_, _Req, _Opts) ->
  {cowboy_websocket, _Req, #{}}.

handle(Req, State) ->
  case cowboy_req:method(Req) of
    <<"GET">> ->
      {ok, Req2} = cowboy_req:reply(200, #{}, <<"Hello, World!">>, Req),
      {ok, Req2, State};
    _ ->
      {ok, Req2} = cowboy_req:reply(404, #{}, <<"Not Found">>, Req),
      {ok, Req2, State}
  end.

terminate(_, _, _) ->
  ok.
```

Next, define the server starting module:

```
-module(simple_http_server).

%% API
-export([start/0, stop/0]).

start() ->
  {ok, _Pid} = cowboy:start_clear(http_listener,
                                  [{port, 8080}],
                                  #{env => #{dispatch => cowboy_router:compile([{'_',
                                         [{'_', simple_handler, []}]}])}}),
  ok.

stop() ->
  cowboy:stop_listener(http_listener).
```

Lastly, create a top-level supervisor to control the web server:

```
-module(web_server_supervisor).
-behaviour(supervisor).

%% API
-export([start_link/0]).

%% supervisor callbacks
-export([init/1]).

start_link() ->
  supervisor:start_link({local, ?MODULE}, ?MODULE, []).

init([]) ->
  {ok, {{one_for_one, 5, 10},
        [{http_server, {simple_http_server, start, []},
        permanent, 5000, worker, [simple_http_server]}]}}.
```

This setup demonstrates the application of OTP for building a fault-tolerant web server. Each component focuses on clear division of tasks, maintaining simplicity while ensuring high reliability and maintainability.

Through these case studies, the OTP framework's versatility becomes clear, enabling efficient design and implementation of various applications while ensuring robustness and fault-tolerance. The consistent application of OTP principles across different domains highlights the framework's strength in creating scalable, maintainable, and resilient systems.

Chapter 8

Building and Running Applications

This chapter covers the complete process of building and running Erlang applications. Topics include creating an initial application, organizing project structure, and compiling and building the software. It addresses configuration, environment setup, deployment, and running applications in production. Additionally, it discusses handling releases, performing upgrades, and scaling applications to meet demand.

8.1 Creating Your First Erlang Application

1. Setting Up Your Erlang Environment

Before creating our first Erlang application, we need to ensure that the Erlang environment is correctly set up. The process involves the following steps:

- Install Erlang OTP: Navigate to the official Erlang website and download the latest version of Erlang OTP suitable for your operating system. Follow the installation instructions provided.
- Verify Installation: Open a terminal and execute the command erl. This command starts the Erlang shell, indicating a successful installation if no errors appear. Exit the shell using q()..

2. Creating the Application Directory

An Erlang application generally follows a specific directory structure. Create a directory for your application and navigate into it:

```
mkdir my_first_app
cd my_first_app
```

3. Defining the Application Structure

Inside your application's root directory, define the standard Erlang application structure:

- src/ - Contains all source files.
- include/ - Holds header files (optional).
- ebin/ - Stores compiled .beam files.

Create these directories using the following commands:

```
mkdir src
mkdir include
mkdir ebin
```

4. Writing Your First Erlang Module

Inside the src/ directory, create an Erlang module named my_first_module.erl:

```
cd src
touch my_first_module.erl
```

Now, open my_first_module.erl in your preferred text editor and write the following code:

```
-module(my_first_module).
-export([start/0]).

start() ->
    io:format("Hello, world!~n").
```

This module consists of:

- -module(my_first_module).: Defines the module name.
- -export([start/0]).: Exports the start/0 function, making it accessible outside the module.
- start/0 function: Prints "Hello, world!" to the console.

5. Compiling the Module

To compile the Erlang module, navigate back to the root directory and start the Erlang shell:

```
cd ..
erl
```

Compile the module with the following command within the Erlang shell:

```
c("src/my_first_module.erl", [{outdir, "ebin"}]).
```

Successful compilation will indicate with:

```
{ok,my_first_module}
```

6. Running Your Application

Now, run your application by calling the start/0 function from my_first_module:

```
my_first_module:start().
```

Output should be:

```
Hello, world!
```

7. Creating an Application Resource File (.app)

Every Erlang application requires an application resource file. Create src/my_first_app.app and add the following contents:

```
{application, my_first_app,
    [
        {description, "My First Erlang Application"},
        {vsn, "1.0"},
        {modules, [my_first_module]},
        {registered, []},
        {applications, [kernel, stdlib]},
        {mod, {my_first_app, []}},
        {env, []}
    ]
}.
```

This file provides Erlang's runtime system with essential information about your application. Key attributes include:

- {description, "My First Erlang Application"}: A brief description.
- {vsn, "1.0"}: Version number of the application.
- {modules, [my_first_module]}: List of modules included.
- {applications, [kernel, stdlib]}: Dependencies.

8. Creating a Supervisor

To manage the lifecycle of processes, define a supervisor module. Create src/my_first_sup.erl:

```
touch src/my_first_sup.erl
```

Edit my_first_sup.erl and add:

```
-module(my_first_sup).
-behaviour(supervisor).

-export([start_link/0, init/1]).

start_link() ->
    supervisor:start_link({local, ?MODULE}, ?MODULE, []).

init(_) ->
    {ok, {{one_for_one, 5, 10},
    [
        {my_first_worker, {my_first_module, start, []},
        permanent, 5000, worker, [my_first_module]}
    ]}}.
```

Important elements:

- -behaviour(supervisor).: Specifies that this module behaves as a supervisor.
- start_link/0: Starts the supervisor.
- init/1: Initializes the supervisor's strategy and child specifications.

9. Running the Supervision Tree

To run the supervision tree, update my_first_app.app with:

```
{mod, {my_first_sup, []}},
```

Recompile the supervisor module:

```
c("src/my_first_sup.erl", [{outdir, "ebin"}]).
```

And start your application:

```
application:start(my_first_app).
```

With these steps, your first Erlang application is successfully created, compiled, and running under a supervision tree, adhering to best practices in the Erlang environment. This provides a strong foundation to build upon, ensuring your applications are robust and maintainable.

8.2 Project Structure and Management

Organizing the structure and management of your Erlang project is critical for maintainability, scalability, and collaboration among multiple developers. An appropriately structured project ensures that the codebase remains understandable, modular, and ready for future extensions. Below, we detail the essential components and best practices for structuring and managing an Erlang project.

Erlang projects typically follow a standardized directory layout, facilitating easier navigation and consistency across projects. The standard layout for an Erlang project includes the following directories:

- src/: Contains all the Erlang source files.
- include/: Used for any header files required by the project.
- ebin/: Holds the compiled .beam files which are the bytecode output of Erlang source files.
- priv/: Contains any static or binary assets needed by the application.
- test/: Holds test scripts and test-related source files.
- deps/: Contains dependencies that the project relies on.
- doc/: Optional directory for documentation.

The src/ directory is the heart of your project; it contains the primary Erlang modules that define the functionality of your application. For example, a project might structure its src/ directory as follows:

```
src/
  app.erl
  app_sup.erl
  app_server.erl
  app_worker.erl
```

app.erl typically defines the application entry point and includes the application callback functions. app_sup.erl acts as the supervisor, managing the lifecycle of processes. app_server.erl and app_worker.erl are server and worker modules, respectively, implementing the business logic.

To manage dependencies, Erlang projects often make use of rebar3, a powerful build tool. rebar3 simplifies dependency management, compilation, and release handling. Here is an example of a typical rebar.config file:

```
{erl_opts, [debug_info]}.
{deps, [
    {cowboy, {git, "https://github.com/ninenines/cowboy.git", {tag, "2.9.0"}}}
]}.
{relx, [
    {release, {
        myapp, "1.0.0",
        [
            myapp,
            sasl
        ]
    }}
]}.
```

In the rebar.config file, you can specify Erlang compilation options using erl_opts. The deps section lists dependencies, specifying each with a tuple containing the repository location and version information. The relx section defines releases and packaging configurations.

A well-organized project structure is complemented by adherence to coding standards. Standard Erlang conventions include using snake_-case for variable names, following appropriate indentation practices, and including module-level and function-level documentation. Here is an example of a well-documented Erlang function:

```
%% @doc
%% Starts the application.
%%
%% @spec start(normal, Args) ->
%% {ok, pid()} |
%% {error, any()}.
start(_Type, _Args) ->
    app_sup:start_link().
```

Testing is paramount in ensuring code quality and robustness. Erlang's standard library includes eunit, a testing framework. Tests are typically placed in the test/ directory and can be executed using rebar3 eunit. Here is an example of a simple unit test:

```
-module(app_test).
-compile([export_all]).
-include_lib("eunit/include/eunit.hrl").

simple_test() ->
    ?assertEqual(4, 2 + 2).
```

When running rebar3 eunit, the output will indicate whether the tests pass or fail:

```
===> Running tests...
  Test simple_test...ok
  All tests passed.
```

Maintaining a consistent directory structure, effective dependency management, adherence to coding standards, and thorough testing are fundamental aspects of managing an Erlang project. These elements collectively ensure that the application is well-prepared for future development and scaling, facilitating team collaboration and long-term maintainability.

8.3 Compiling and Building Applications

In this section, we focus on the essential steps required to compile and build Erlang applications. This involves translating the high-level language into executable code and organizing that code in a structure best suited for deployment and execution. We will explore tools and commands provided by the Erlang/OTP (Open Telecom Platform) and other supplementary utilities to facilitate this process.

Compiling an Erlang application involves turning source files, which are written in the .erl file extension, into bytecode files with the .beam extension. This bytecode is the intermediate representation that the Erlang virtual machine (BEAM) executes.

```
-module(sample).
-export([start/0]).

start() ->
    io:format("Hello, Erlang!~n").
```

To compile this module, navigate to the directory containing sample.erl and execute the following command in the Erlang shell:

```
1> c(sample).
{ok,sample}
```

After successful compilation, you will notice a file named sample.beam in the directory. This file contains the bytecode that can be executed by the BEAM virtual machine.

Rebar3 is a widely used build tool that assists in managing dependencies, compiling code, and packaging applications. To utilize Rebar3, follow these steps:

1. Install Rebar3 by downloading the binary from the official repository or using package managers such as Homebrew on macOS:

```
brew install rebar3
```

2. Create a new Erlang project:

```
rebar3 new app myapp
```

This command creates a directory structure:

```
myapp/
  _build/
  config/
    sys.config
  src/
    myapp.app.src
    myapp_sup.erl
  rebar.config
```

The src/ directory is where .erl files reside, and rebar.config is the configuration file for Rebar3. The .app.src file defines the application structure and metadata.

To compile the project using Rebar3, execute the following command within the myapp directory:

```
rebar3 compile
```

Rebar3 compiles all .erl files in the src/ directory and places the .beam files in the _build/default/lib/myapp/ebin/ directory.

To facilitate build automation and continuous integration, integrating these commands in automated scripts (e.g., Makefile or CI/CD pipeline scripts) ensures repeatability and consistency. A basic Makefile for an Erlang project might include:

```
.PHONY: all compile clean

all: compile

compile:
  rebar3 compile

clean:
  rebar3 clean
```

This configuration allows developers to execute make commands:

```
make
make clean
```

Advanced build configurations can involve:

- Dependent libraries specified in rebar.config:

```
{deps, [
    {cowboy, "2.7.0"}
]}.
```

- Customized compilation options, such as specifying different profiles for development, testing, and production environments.
- Integrating unit tests automatically to ensure code stability through rebar3 ct (Common Test) or rebar3 eunit commands.

Algorithm 1: Erlang Application Compilation Process

Data: Source files in src/ directory
Result: Compiled .beam files in _build/ directory

```
Initialize Rebar3 in the project directory;
foreach .erl file in src/ directory do
    Compile the file to .beam format using Rebar3;
    if compilation fails then
        Output error and halt build process;
Move .beam files to _build/default/lib/{app_name}/ebin/;
```

Building complex Erlang applications often involves splitting the project into smaller, manageable sub-applications or modules, each with its own directory and rebar.config file. This modular approach supports separation of concerns, better dependency management, and easier codebase navigation.

As applications grow in size and complexity, automating the build and deployment pipeline becomes indispensable. Continuous Integration (CI) platforms such as Jenkins, GitLab CI, or GitHub Actions can be configured to trigger the build process upon code changes, ensuring that the latest codebase is always compiled and ready for deployment.

Using Docker for containerized builds is another best practice. A basic Dockerfile for building an Erlang application might look like:

```
FROM erlang:23-alpine

WORKDIR /app

COPY . /app

RUN rebar3 compile

CMD ["rebar3", "shell"]
```

This setup ensures a consistent build environment, independent of the underlying host system. Containerization also simplifies the process of deploying Erlang applications across different environments.

Configuring the build to support different environments ensures that the application can be reliably built and deployed in various stages, from development to production. This detailed understanding of Erlang application compilation and build process provides a foundation for creating robust, efficient, and easily maintainable Erlang software.

8.4 Configuration and Environment Setup

Effective configuration and environment setup are critical components in the lifecycle of an Erlang application. Proper management of configuration files and environment variables ensures that the application behaves as expected across various environments such as development, testing, and production. This section delves into the details of configuring your Erlang application using configuration files and environment variables, structuring your configuration for better maintainability, and setting up environments for smooth deployment.

Configuration in Erlang is typically handled through config files, often written in Erlang term format. An example of a sys.config file might look like this:

```
[
  {my_app,
    [
      {database, "postgresql"},
      {db_host, "localhost"},
      {db_port, 5432},
      {db_username, "admin"},
      {db_password, "secret"}
    ]
  }
].
```

In this example, configuration parameters for my_app are defined, including database settings such as db_host, db_port, db_username, and db_password. These parameters can be accessed within the application at runtime using the application:get_env/2 function from the application module:

```
DbHost = application:get_env(my_app, db_host),
DbPort = application:get_env(my_app, db_port),
DbUsername = application:get_env(my_app, db_username),
DbPassword = application:get_env(my_app, db_password).
```

By using application:get_env/2, you ensure that your application retrieves its configuration information from the appropriate source, typically the sys.config file or environment-specific configuration files included during the runtime.

Environment variables are another essential component for managing different settings per environment. Erlang leverages the os module which provides functions to retrieve environment variables. These can be integrated into the application to allow variability in configurations without changing the codebase or the configuration files. For example:

```
DbHost = os:getenv("DB_HOST"),
DbPort = os:getenv("DB_PORT"),
DbUsername = os:getenv("DB_USERNAME"),
DbPassword = os:getenv("DB_PASSWORD").
```

These environment variables can be set in the system according to the environment, for instance, setting different values on a production machine versus a development machine.

To structure multiple environment configurations, consider having distinct configuration files for each environment:

- sys_dev.config for development
- sys_test.config for testing
- sys_prod.config for production

Each of these files would contain pertinent configurations applicable to the respective environments:

```
%% sys_dev.config
[
    {my_app,
        [
            {database, "postgresql"},
            {db_host, "localhost"},
            {db_port, 5432},
            {db_username, "dev"},
            {db_password, "devpass"}
        ]
    }
].
```

```
%% sys_test.config
[
    {my_app,
        [
            {database, "postgresql"},
            {db_host, "test.local"},
            {db_port, 5432},
```

```
            {db_username, "tester"},
            {db_password, "testpass"}
        ]
    }
].
```

```
%% sys_prod.config
[
    {my_app,
        [
            {database, "postgresql"},
            {db_host, "prod.server"},
            {db_port, 5432},
            {db_username, "admin"},
            {db_password, "prodpass"}
        ]
    }
].
```

These files can be specified when starting the Erlang runtime system using the -config flag:

```
erl -config sys_dev
erl -config sys_test
erl -config sys_prod
```

This practice allows you to tailor your application's behavior according to the environment in which it is running without altering the main codebase or involving manual changes.

Additionally, there are tools like rebar3 that facilitate the configuration and environment setup in a more sophisticated manner. rebar3 can package and deploy configurations based on the profiles defined in its configuration:

```
{profiles,
    [{dev, [{relx, [{dev_mode, true}]}]},
     {test, [{relx, [{dev_mode, false}, {include_src, false}]}]},
     {prod, [{relx, [{dev_mode, false}, {include_src, false}, {include_erts, true}]}]}]
}.
```

Having a profile-based approach helps maintain clarity between different environment setups, ensuring that proper configurations are applied during the build and deployment process.

Thoroughly validating your configurations in each environment is essential. Testing should involve simulated environments that mimic the production as closely as possible. This ensures that all configurations regarding databases, external services, and internal application settings are thoroughly vetted before going live.

With a robust configuration and environment setup, the application gains flexibility and maintainability, enhancing its ability to adapt to changing requirements and environments with minimal disruptions. The focus should be on keeping the configurations organized, easily accessible, and sufficiently abstracted to avoid frequent modifications to the core application code.

8.5 Deploying Erlang Applications

Deploying Erlang applications involves several steps to ensure that the software can efficiently transition from the development environment to the production environment. This process not only includes transferring the application code but also configuring the application to run in the new environment, managing dependencies, and ensuring that necessary system resources are appropriately allocated.

Setting Up the Deployment Environment

Before deploying an Erlang application, it is essential to prepare the target environment. This preparation includes ensuring that Erlang/OTP is installed on the target systems. You can verify the installed version by executing:

```
erl -version
```

The output will generally indicate the installed version of Erlang/OTP. Next, it's essential to synchronize application dependencies between the development and production environments. This synchronization can be handled through build tools such as Rebar3.

Building the Release

Rebar3 is an essential build tool for Erlang projects, which simplifies the creation of releases. First, you must define your project's dependencies and configuration in the rebar.config file.

```
{deps, [
    {cowboy, "2.8.0"},
    {jsx, "2.9.0"}
]}.

{relx, [{release, {my_app, "0.1.0"},
          [my_app, sasl]},
         {dev_mode, true},
         {include_erts, false}]}.
```

Run the following command to generate the release:

```
rebar3 release
```

This command compiles your application and generates a release package in the _build/default/rel/ directory. The release contains all the necessary files to run the application, including the Erlang runtime system (ERTS) if specified.

Transferring the Release

Once the release is built, you need to transfer it to the target production system. This transfer can be achieved through various methods such as SCP, FTP, or other file transfer protocols. For example:

```
scp -r _build/default/rel/my_app user@remotehost:/path/to/deploy/
```

Ensure that the target directory on the production system has the appropriate permissions set to allow the application to run.

Configuring the Application

After transferring the release, the next step is to configure the application. Configuration files, typically located in the config directory of the release, might include sys.config and vm.args.

```
% sys.config
{kernel, [
    {inet_dist_listen_min, 9100},
    {inet_dist_listen_max, 9200}
]}.

% vm.args
-name my_app_node@hostname
-setcookie my_secret_cookie
```

These configurations control various runtime parameters, such as the node name and cookie for distributed Erlang nodes.

Starting the Application

To start the application on the target system, navigate to the release directory and use the following command:

```
./bin/my_app console
```

Alternatively, you can start the application in detached mode, suitable for a production environment:

```
./bin/my_app start
```

You can check the status of the application with:

```
./bin/my_app ping
```

This command pings the running node, and if successful, the output will be:

```
pong
```

Monitoring and Logging

Monitoring and logging configurations are crucial for maintaining the application in production. Ensure that logging is adequately set up in the sys.config file:

```
{logger, [
    {handler, default, logger_std_h, #{level => info}}
]}.
```

Logs are typically stored in the log directory under the release directory. Monitoring tools such as observer can be utilized for real-time inspection of node activities:

```
observer:start().
```

This command starts the Observer tool, which provides a graphical overview of the system's processes, memory, and performance metrics.

Integrating these steps ensures that deploying Erlang applications is seamless and robust, catering to the requirements of a production environment.

8.6 Running Applications in Production

Deploying an Erlang application into a production environment requires adherence to several best practices to ensure reliability, performance, and maintainability. This section details the process, covering aspects such as starting the application, managing system resources, monitoring runtime performance, and establishing effective logging and error-handling mechanisms.

Starting the Application

In a production setting, the application should be started using the release built by the Erlang/OTP release handling tools. This ensures that all dependencies, configurations, and environment variables are correctly set up.

```
$ ./_build/default/rel/myapp/bin/myapp start
```

This command initializes and starts the application as a background process. It leverages the release configuration to ensure that all necessary components are loaded and all preconditions are met.

Managing System Resources

Efficiently managing system resources is critical in a production environment. Erlang's lightweight process model and built-in OTP (Open Telecom Platform) behaviors aid considerably in resource management. However, it is vital to configure the VM (Virtual Machine) settings appropriately:

- +S sets the number of scheduler threads.
- +K true enables kernel poll for better I/O handling.
- +A configures the number of asynchronous threads.

Example configuration:

```
$ ./_build/default/rel/myapp/bin/myapp start \
  -smp enable +S 4 +K true +A 10
```

Monitoring Runtime Performance

Monitoring the running application is essential to detect and resolve issues promptly. Use tools such as eper (Erlang Performance Monitoring) and observer. The observer module in Erlang provides a graphical interface for monitoring the system.

```
% Run in the shell to start observer
1> observer:start().
```

For automated monitoring, you can set up metrics reporting through folsom or exometer. These tools allow you to monitor CPU load, memory usage, process counts, and other critical metrics.

Establishing Effective Logging

Proper logging is indispensable for diagnosing production issues. Use the logger module to implement structured logging. Logger configurations are typically defined in the sys.config file.

Example sys.config entry:

```
{logger, [
    {handler, default, logger_std_h,
        #{level => info, config => #{type => standard_io}}},
    {handler, file_log, logger_disk_log_h,
        #{config => #{file => "log/myapp.log", level => debug}}}
]}.
```

This configuration logs standard output at the info level and writes debug logs to a file.

Handling Errors

Robust error handling ensures that the system recovers gracefully from failures. Use OTP design principles such as supervisors and gen_-server callbacks to implement fault tolerance.

Example supervisor implementation:

```
-module(myapp_sup).
-behaviour(supervisor).

-export([start_link/0, init/1]).

start_link() ->
    supervisor:start_link({local, ?MODULE}, ?MODULE, []).

init([]) ->
    RestartStrategy = one_for_one,
    MaxRestarts = 3,
    MaxSeconds = 60,
    ChildSpecs = [
        {myapp_worker, {myapp_worker, start_link, []},
            permanent, 5000, worker, [myapp_worker]}
    ],
    {ok, {RestartStrategy, MaxRestarts, MaxSeconds, ChildSpecs}}.
```

This example outlines a basic supervisor configuration that restarts the worker process up to three times within a minute if it crashes.

By carefully managing the start-up process, system resources, monitoring runtime performance, logging, and error handling, one can ensure that an Erlang application runs reliably and efficiently in production environments. Proper configuration and adherence to OTP principles are necessary to handle the complexities of production deployment seamlessly.

8.7 Release Handling and Upgrades

In Erlang, managing software releases and performing upgrades is a crucial aspect of maintaining robust and scalable applications. Given the distributed nature of Erlang systems, ensuring seamless upgrades without downtime is essential. This section delves into the concepts, tools, and methodologies involved in release handling and upgrades.

Release Basics

A release in Erlang is a packaged version of an application or a set of applications. It contains everything needed to run the application, including the Erlang runtime, compiled code, configuration files, and scripts for starting, stopping, and upgrading the application.

- **Release Versioning:** Erlang follows a versioning scheme for releases. A typical version string is in the form X.Y.Z, where X is the major version, Y is the minor version, and Z denotes the patch level.
- **Release Configuration:** The release is defined using a .rel file, which specifies the applications included in the release, their versions, and the order in which they should start.

Creating a Release

To create a release, you need to use the release resource file. An example of a basic .rel file is shown below:

```
{release, {"myapp", "1.0.0"},
 [{erts, "10.3"},
  {kernel, "6.5"},
  {stdlib, "3.10"},
  {myapp, "1.0"}]
}.
```

This file defines a release named myapp with version 1.0.0 and includes the specified versions of the Erlang runtime system (erts), kernel, standard libraries, and the application itself.

Building Releases

Erlang provides a tool called relx for building releases. To build the release, you need to configure relx by creating a relx.config file:

```
{release,
  {myapp, "1.0.0"},
  [kernel, stdlib, myapp]}.

{extended_start_script, true}.
```

With the configuration in place, you can build the release by running:

```
$ rebar3 release
```

This command compiles the application and packages it into a release that can be deployed and run on an Erlang runtime system.

Handling Upgrades

Upgrading an Erlang application involves creating and applying patches to the existing release. This allows for changes in code, configuration, or both without stopping the system. Erlang's release handling capabilities support hot code upgrades, which are critical for high-availability systems.

Upgrade File

An upgrade file, often referred to as a .appup file, specifies how to upgrade and downgrade the application. Below is an example myapp.appup file for version 1.0.1 upgrading to 1.0.2:

```
{"1.0.2",
 [{"1.0.1", [{update, my_mod, {advanced, []}}]}],
 [{"1.0.1", [{remove, my_mod, {advanced, []}}]}]
}.
```

This file defines the steps needed to upgrade from version 1.0.1 to 1.0.2 and vice-versa. The update and remove directives indicate how the module should be handled during the upgrade or downgrade process.

Creating a Release Upgrade

Once the .appup file is defined, the next step is to generate a release upgrade file, commonly known as relup. This can be achieved using the systools:make_relup/3 function:

```
systools:make_relup("myapp-1.0.2", ["myapp-1.0.1"], ["myapp-1.0.0"]).
```

This command produces a myapp-1.0.2.relup file, which incorporates the upgrade and downgrade instructions.

Applying the Upgrade

To apply the upgrade, first copy the new release and the relup file to the target system. Then initiate the upgrade using the release_handler module:

```
release_handler:unpack_release("myapp-1.0.2").
release_handler:install_release("1.0.2").
release_handler:make_permanent("1.0.2").
```

Unpacking extracts the release files, installing activates the new release, and making it permanent finalizes the upgrade.

Hot Code Swapping

Erlang's ability to handle hot code swapping is one of its standout features. This process allows for module upgrades without taking the system offline. The VM maintains two versions of any active module at any given time, ensuring smooth transitions.

Loading New Code

New code is loaded into the system using the code module:

```
code:load_file(my_mod).
```

This command loads the new version of the my_mod module, and existing processes start using the new code from their next call.

Handling State Changes

Upgrade paths often require managing state changes. The gen_server behavior includes mechanisms for handling such upgrades through the code_change callback:

```
code_change(_OldVsn, State, _Extra) ->
    {ok, State}.
```

This function allows state transformation between versions, ensuring that live processes can adapt to the new code seamlessly.

Release handling and upgrades in Erlang demand careful planning and precision. Building and working with releases involve configuration management, understanding versioning, and leveraging tools like relx and the release_handler module. Upgrading a system showcases Erlang's powerful capabilities in hot code swapping and maintaining high availability, both essential for enterprise-level applications.

8.8 Scaling Applications

Scaling Erlang applications involves adapting the software to handle an increased number of requests and processing larger volumes of data without sacrificing performance or reliability. Scaling can be performed horizontally, by adding more nodes to an Erlang cluster, or vertically, by increasing the computational power or resources of the existing nodes. Key concepts include load balancing, distribution, node communication, and resource management.

Erlang's architecture, which natively supports concurrency and fault tolerance, is well-suited for scalable applications. Processes in Erlang are lightweight and isolated, allowing easy spawning and management of many processes simultaneously. This inherent design facilitates parallel execution and efficient resource utilization across multiple cores and nodes.

Horizontal Scaling

Horizontal scaling entails adding more Erlang nodes to a distributed system. Each node runs an instance of the Erlang runtime system and can communicate with other nodes in the cluster. This approach enhances the system's capacity to process a larger number of parallel tasks.

```
% Start an Erlang node
$ erl -sname node1

% Connect to another node
(node1@hostname)1> net_adm:ping('node2@hostname').
pong
```

Nodes in an Erlang distributed system share no memory and communicate via message passing. This approach avoids the complications of shared state and allows the system to scale by simply adding more nodes. Proper node communication and management are essential.

```
Node1 > net_adm:ping('node2@hostname').
pong
```

Load Balancing

Effective load balancing ensures that the workload is evenly distributed across all nodes in the system. One common technique involves a process registry, which records where processes are running and distributes new requests accordingly. The built-in module pg2 can be employed to manage process groups and perform load balancing.

```
% Create a new process group
```

```
pg2:create(my_group).

% Join a process to the group
pg2:join(my_group, self()).

% Send a message to all members of the group
pg2:send(my_group, {do_work, Request}).
```

Load balancing can also be achieved using third-party tools such as HAProxy, which can intelligently route traffic to different nodes based on their current load and response time.

Node Communication and Monitoring

Erlang nodes use the distributed Erlang protocol for communication. Nodes can be monitored and managed using the riak_core library or similar tools. Monitoring includes checking the status of each node, the message queue lengths, and the uptime.

```
% Monitor the local node
slave:start('node2@hostname', erlang).

% Check the status of the remote node
rpc:call('node2@hostname', erlang, node, []).
```

Implementing a monitoring strategy involves using system telemetry to capture metrics such as CPU usage, memory consumption, and process counts.

Resource Management

Effective resource management ensures that each node operates efficiently. This can involve controlling process limits, optimizing memory usage, and managing I/O operations. Configurations can be adjusted in the Erlang runtime system to better allocate resources. For instance, the +P flag sets the maximum number of simultaneous processes.

```
% Start an Erlang node with a higher process limit
$ erl +P 134217727
```

Optimizing memory usage might involve configuring garbage collection parameters or tuning specific application code to avoid memory leaks.

Handling System Bottlenecks

Identifying and addressing system bottlenecks is critical in scaling applications. Profiling tools such as eprof and fprof can be used to pinpoint performance issues and areas that require optimization.

```
% Start profiling
eprof:start().
```

```
% Start tracing a specific process
eprof:trace(Process).

% Analyze the results
eprof:analyze().

% Stop profiling
eprof:stop().
```

Case Study: Scaling a Real-world Application

Consider a web application where an increase in user traffic is anticipated. A scaling strategy might involve:

- Load testing the current system using a tool like Tsung to identify the current capacity and bottlenecks.
- Adding additional nodes to the cluster to distribute the load more evenly.
- Implementing a load balancer to intelligently route requests to the least loaded nodes.
- Monitoring the nodes using system tools and adjusting configurations for optimal performance.
- Employing database replication and sharding techniques if the database becomes a bottleneck.

In Erlang, scaling is not merely adding more hardware; it involves a careful, systematic approach to ensure that each part of the system can handle increased load efficiently while maintaining reliability and performance.

Chapter 9

Testing and Debugging

This chapter focuses on testing and debugging in Erlang. It covers unit testing with EUnit, property-based testing with PropEr, and integration testing. Additionally, it discusses load and performance testing, debugging tools and techniques, using the Erlang Observer, and profiling and optimization. The goal is to provide comprehensive strategies for ensuring robust and efficient Erlang applications.

9.1 Introduction to Testing in Erlang

Testing is a critical phase in the software development lifecycle, ensuring that an application meets its specified requirements and performs reliably in real-world conditions. In Erlang, testing takes on a particular importance due to the concurrent and distributed nature of most applications written in the language. Consequently, a thorough understanding of Erlang's testing methodologies is indispensable for any proficient developer. This section introduces foundational concepts and tools for testing in Erlang, establishing the groundwork for more advanced topics discussed later in the chapter.

Erlang offers a rich set of tools for testing various aspects of an application, from unit tests and property-based tests to integration and performance tests. The primary tools we will focus on include EUnit for unit testing, PropEr for property-based testing, and Common Test for integration testing.

EUnit is Erlang's built-in unit testing framework. It enables developers to write tests alongside their code, promoting an approach where testing becomes an integral part of the development process. Unit tests in EUnit are typically small and focused on testing individual functions or modules in isolation.

PropEr (Property-based testing) is a testing technique where instead of writing specific examples as tests, the developer specifies properties that the functions should satisfy. PropEr then automatically generates test cases that try to falsify these properties. This method can uncover edge cases that might not be immediately apparent through conventional unit tests.

Common Test is Erlang's application for writing extensive test suites for integration testing. It excels in scenarios where different components of a system must be tested together to ensure they function correctly when integrated.

When introducing testing in Erlang, one must first consider the specifications and requirements of the project to decide the appropriate testing strategies. The testing environment should closely mirror the production environment to ensure the reliability of the tests.

```
-module(my_module).
-compile([export_all]).

% Function to add two numbers
add(X, Y) -> X + Y.

% Sample EUnit test
my_module_test_() ->
    [
        ?_assertEqual(5, add(2, 3))
    ].
```

In the example above, my_module is defined with a single function add/2 that adds two numbers. The corresponding EUnit test my_module_test_() verifies that the add function works correctly for the given input.

Executing this test prints the following output, verifying the correctness of the addition function:

```
EUnit test...
my_module: my_module_test_...ok
All tests passed.
```

Property-based testing with PropEr involves specifying properties instead of particular test cases. Consider the property that the addition of two numbers should commutatively give the same result:

```
-module(proper_test).
-compile([export_all]).
-include_lib("proper/include/proper.hrl").

prop_add_commutative() ->
    ?FORALL({X, Y}, {integer(), integer()},
        add(X, Y) =:= add(Y, X)).
```

By calling the function prop_add_commutative/0, PropEr verifies the commutative property for a wide range of randomly generated integer pairs:

```
prop_add_commutative: Starting...
....
prop_add_commutative: Passed after 100 tests

1 property passed.
```

In more complex applications, where multiple components interact, integrating these components can lead to unforeseen issues.

```
-module(integ_test).
-compile([export_all]).
-include_lib("common_test/include/ct.hrl").

% Sample integration test suite
init_per_suite(Config) ->
    % Setup code
    Config.

end_per_suite(Config) ->
    % Teardown code
    ok.

test_addition(Config) ->
    ?assertEqual(5, my_module:add(2, 3)).
```

In the above example, integ_test uses Common Test to provide a more extensive testing strategy. Each test case is executed within the context of a test suite, allowing for setup and teardown processes via init_per_suite/1 and end_per_suite/1 respectively.

Running integration tests yields detailed outputs that inform developers of the results for each test case:

```
%%% integ_test_SUITE: test_addition (Module: integ_test) %%%
%%% integ_test_SUITE ==> test_addition: OK, 6 milliseconds %%%
\#\#\# All tests passed. ###
```

For testing to be effective in Erlang, tests should be comprehensive, focusing not only on the correctness of the code but also on its reliability, performance, and ability to handle concurrent operations.

9.2 Unit Testing with EUnit

EUnit is a lightweight unit testing framework designed to streamline the process of testing Erlang code. EUnit is highly integrated into Erlang and offers a set of macros that allow developers to define test cases closely within their code. This section explores the fundamental elements required to effectively create and execute unit tests in Erlang using EUnit.

To begin with, consider a simple module, math_utils, which contains basic arithmetic functions. The module is structured as shown in the following example:

```
-module(math_utils).
-export([add/2, subtract/2, multiply/2, divide/2]).

add(X, Y) -> X + Y.
subtract(X, Y) -> X - Y.
multiply(X, Y) -> X * Y.
divide(X, 0) -> {error, divide_by_zero};
divide(X, Y) -> X / Y.
```

To write unit tests for this module, create a test file named math_utils_-tests.erl. This test module will contain different test cases that validate the functions in the math_utils module. Enable EUnit by including the necessary header:

```
-module(math_utils_tests).
-include_lib("eunit/include/eunit.hrl").
```

Next, define the test cases within the module. EUnit allows us to define tests using _test() suffix with the functions. Here's how you can structure and write test cases for each function:

```
math_utils_add_test() ->
  ?assertEqual(5, math_utils:add(2, 3)),
  ?assertEqual(-1, math_utils:add(2, -3)),
  ?assertEqual(0, math_utils:add(0, 0)).

math_utils_subtract_test() ->
  ?assertEqual(1, math_utils:subtract(3, 2)),
  ?assertEqual(5, math_utils:subtract(2, -3)),
  ?assertEqual(0, math_utils:subtract(0, 0)).

math_utils_multiply_test() ->
  ?assertEqual(6, math_utils:multiply(2, 3)),
  ?assertEqual(-6, math_utils:multiply(2, -3)),
  ?assertEqual(0, math_utils:multiply(2, 0)).

math_utils_divide_test() ->
  ?assertEqual(2.0, math_utils:divide(6, 3)),
  ?assertEqual({error, divide_by_zero}, math_utils:divide(6, 0)).
```

Test assertions within EUnit are made using macros such as ?assertEqual that compare the expected outcome with the actual result. The macro will raise an error if the values do not match, thus marking the test as failed.

Once the test functions are defined, you can compile and run tests from the Erlang shell as follows:

```
c(math_utils).
c(math_utils_tests).
eunit:test(math_utils_tests).
```

The output of the test execution will look like:

```
========================== EUnit ==========================
module 'math_utils_tests'
  math_utils_tests: math_utils_add_test...ok
  math_utils_tests: math_utils_subtract_test...ok
  math_utils_tests: math_utils_multiply_test...ok
  math_utils_tests: math_utils_divide_test...ok
  [done in 0.019 s]
============================================================
```

EUnit also supports test fixtures setup and teardown to prepare the environment before tests and cleaning up afterward. Use setup/2 and teardown/1 macros for this purpose:

```
math_utils_fixture_test_() ->
  {setup, fun() -> io:format("Setting up~n") end,
   fun(_Result) -> io:format("Tearing down~n") end,
   fun() ->
     ?assertEqual(5, math_utils:add(2, 3)),
     ?assertEqual(1, math_utils:subtract(3, 2))
   end}.
```

This test introduces setup and teardown methods ensuring that any resource is initialized and cleaned up properly before and after the tests run. Executing the above test will result in output inclusive of the setup and teardown steps:

```
Setting up
Tearing down
```

Further, EUnit macros contribute to facilitating complex testing scenarios by supporting list-based tests. Here, groups of tests can be collected into a single test set:

```
math_utils_all_tests_test_() ->
  [math_utils_add_test,
   math_utils_subtract_test,
   math_utils_multiply_test,
   math_utils_divide_test].
```

EUnit's flexibility also allows parameterized testing, where test cases are composed using given parameters:

```
math_utils_parameterized_test() ->
  ?assertEqual(TestData, ExpectedResult)
  || {TestData, ExpectedResult} <- math_utils:get_test_data().

get_test_data() -> [{2, 3, 5}, {3, 4, 7}, {5, 6, 11}].
```

By defining clean test structures and comprehensive cases, EUnit significantly aids in maintaining high-quality, error-free code. Through methodical implementation of these testing principles, developers can ensure robust validation of their Erlang modules.

9.3 Property-Based Testing with PropEr

Property-based testing extends beyond the capabilities of traditional unit tests by focusing on the properties that functions should satisfy. PropEr, a powerful testing tool for Erlang, enables specifying these properties and automatically generating diverse test cases to validate them.

PropEr requires defining properties using logical statements. These properties are then tested by exploring a vast combination of input values to ensure comprehensive coverage. Unlike unit tests, which check specific cases, property-based testing makes broad generalizations to ensure correctness across an entire input space.

First, integrate PropEr into your project by adding it as a dependency. Ensure your rebar.config file includes the necessary configuration:

```
{deps, [
    {proper, "git://github.com/proper-testing/proper.git", {branch, "master"}}
]}.
```

Once PropEr is incorporated, it's crucial to understand its foundational constructs, such as generating values and defining properties.

Generating Values: PropEr includes various built-in generators to create a diversity of data types. Use proper:pick/1 to sample values from standard generators such as integers, atoms, lists, and more. Below is an example:

```
proper:pick(integer()).
proper:pick(atom()).
proper:pick(list(integer())).
```

Custom Generators: For more complex data structures, define custom generators using Erlang functions and PropEr combinators. The let/2 combinator facilitates creating new generators from existing ones:

```
module(my_generator).
-export([gen_tree/0]).

gen_tree() ->
    ?LET(Tree, tree(integer()),
         {Tree, sum(Tree)}).

tree(LeafType) ->
    ?SUCHTHAT(T, T /= [],
              ?ONEOF([empty, {node, LeafType, tree(LeafType), tree(LeafType)}])).
```

Above, gen_tree/0 defines a tree structure generator, combining integers within a tree with ?LET to also compute the sum of tree nodes. Utilize ?SUCHTHAT, ensuring non-empty trees.

Defining Properties: Base property definitions on logical expressions that must hold true across all generated test cases. Use proper:forall/2 to test properties:

```
prop_reverse() ->
    ?FORALL(L, list(integer()),
            lists:reverse(lists:reverse(L)) == L).
```

In prop_reverse/0, the property asserts double reversing any list results in the original list. PropEr generates multiple lists, confirming this property holds each time.

Running Property Tests: Execute property tests within test modules using PropEr's proper:quickcheck/1 and proper:quickcheck/2. Embed results display for comprehensive assessment:

```
proper:quickcheck(my_module:prop_reverse()).
```

To organize tests effectively, employ EUnit integration for seamless inclusion in automated test suites:

```
-module(my_test).
-include_lib("proper/include/proper.hrl").
-include_lib("eunit/include/eunit.hrl").

reverse_test() ->
    proper:quickcheck(my_module:prop_reverse()).
```

Integrate with EUnit, executing reverse_test/0 as part of the test suite automatically.

Shrinking: PropEr not only finds failing cases but attempts to minimize them for debugging. This shrinking process isolates the simplest test case causing a failure, aiding in swift identification and rectification of underlying issues. Consider the below failing property under particular conditions:

```
prop_map_filter() ->
    ?FORALL(L, list(integer()),
            lists:map(fun(X) -> X + 1 end,
                    lists:filter(fun(X) -> X rem 2 == 0 end, L)) == lists:filter(fun(X)
                        -> X rem 2 == 0 end, lists:map(fun(X) -> X + 1 end, L))).
```

If this property fails, PropEr starts by identifying minimal failing lists (e.g., /[0]/, /[0, 1]/), simplifying the debugging process.

Integrating with PropEr:

- Consistently define properties relevant to critical functionalities.
- Utilize generators to encompass a broad spectrum of input data.
- Leverage shrinking for efficient error isolation.

Property-based testing with PropEr underscores an effective methodology for validating Erlang functions' robustness, ensuring broad input data coverage and streamlined debugging through minimal failing test cases.

9.4 Integration Testing

Integration testing in Erlang involves verifying the interactions between various components within your application. This ensures that individual units function correctly when combined and that dependencies work in unison. This process identifies issues arising from the integration of smaller modules, which may not be apparent through unit testing alone.

To conduct integration testing effectively in Erlang, several best practices and tools can be employed. We'll discuss defining test scenarios, automating tests, and utilizing common tools such as Common Test.

Defining Test Scenarios

A well-defined test scenario is crucial for successful integration testing. Integration test scenarios simulate real-world cases where different modules interact. The following steps outline an efficient approach to defining these scenarios:

- Identify all modules participating in the integration.

- Understand and document the communication patterns between these modules.
- Determine the input and expected output for each module and the system as a whole.
- Define edge cases and error conditions that need to be tested.

Automating Integration Tests

Automation is essential for efficient integration testing, providing a repeatable and consistent testing process. Erlang's Common Test framework is specialized for this purpose. Below, we explore the integration of Common Test into an Erlang project.

First, we configure the test environment by creating a test directory within your project structure:

```
$ mkdir test
$ mkdir test/config
$ mkdir test/logs
```

Next, we create a test configuration file, test.config, under the test/config directory. This file specifies the settings for the test environment. An example test.config might look like this:

```
[
 {integration_test, [
   {modules, [my_app_module1, my_app_module2]},
   {run_timeout, 10000}
 ]}
].
```

In the test directory, define test suites for the modules that need integration testing. Consider an example test suite for modules my_app_module1 and my_app_module2:

```
-module(integration_test).
-compile(export_all).
-include_lib("common_test/include/ct.hrl").

init_per_suite(Config) ->
    [{dir, ?config(data_dir, Config)}].

end_per_suite(_Config) ->
    ok.

init_per_testcase(_TestCase, Config) ->
    Config.

end_per_testcase(_TestCase, _Config) ->
    ok.

all() ->
```

```
    [integration_test_case].

integration_test_case(Config) ->
    % Start the modules
    my_app_module1:start_link(),
    my_app_module2:start_link(),

    % Send test messages
    my_app_module1:send_message(self(), {hello, world}),
    receive
        {hello, world} -> ?assert(true);
        _Other -> ?assert(false)
    after 5000 ->
        ?assert(false)
    end,

    % Ensure proper shutdown
    my_app_module1:stop(),
    my_app_module2:stop().
```

The init_per_suite/1 and end_per_suite/1 functions set up and tear down the resources needed for all test cases in the suite. The all/0 function lists all the test cases within the suite. Each test case follows a pattern of starting the modules, performing interactions, and checking the outcomes.

Execution of Integration Tests

Execute your Common Test test suite from the Erlang shell using the following command:

```
(ct:run_test([{dir, "test"}])).
```

Alternatively, due to the Common Test framework's integration with rebar3, you can run the tests using:

```
$ rebar3 ct
```

```
======================== EUnit ========================
my_app_module1_test: integration_test_case... [OK]
[done in 0.243 s]
=======================================================
```

Best Practices and Tips

When writing integration tests, ensure that your tests are isolated, meaning that the outcome of one test shouldn't affect another. This can be managed through proper initialization and cleanup procedures. Additionally, strive to cover various interaction patterns, including normal operations and failure scenarios, to build a comprehensive test suite.

Using mocking in integration tests can sometimes be necessary to simulate interactions with external services or components that are not available within the test environment. Erlang's meck library can be used for creating such mocks.

The configuration of your test environment should align closely with the production environment to ensure that any integration issues are detected early.

By focusing on thorough scenario definitions, automation with Common Test, and following best practices, integration testing will significantly contribute to the reliability and robustness of your Erlang applications, ensuring seamless cooperation between different modules and components.

9.5 Load and Performance Testing

Load and performance testing are critical aspects of ensuring that an Erlang application can handle the anticipated workload under real-world conditions. These tests help identify bottlenecks, resource limitations, and system weaknesses. This section will delve into techniques and tools for performing load and performance testing in Erlang.

1. Concepts of Load and Performance Testing

Load testing involves evaluating the behavior of the system under increased load, simulating user activity or message volume to ensure it can perform under peak conditions. Performance testing, on the other hand, focuses on assessing the responsiveness, speed, and scalability of the system. Both forms of testing are crucial for identifying performance degradations, ensuring the application meets performance benchmarks, and providing a seamless user experience.

2. Tools for Load Testing

Multiple tools can be employed for load testing in Erlang, each with its strengths. A popular choice is Tsung, which is a highly scalable multi-protocol distributed load testing tool. Tsung can simulate thousands of simultaneous users and is capable of testing various protocols including HTTP, WebDAV, SOAP, PostgreSQL, and Jabber/XMPP.

2.1 Setting Up Tsung

To use Tsung for load testing, start by installing Tsung:

```
sudo apt-get install tsung
```

Next, configure Tsung by creating an XML configuration file that defines the users, sessions, and targets of the load test. Here is an example configuration:

```
<tsung loglevel="notice">
    <clients>
        <client host="localhost" use_controller_vm="true" />
    </clients>
    <servers>
        <server host="your_server_host" port="80" type="tcp" />
    </servers>
    <load>
        <arrivalphase phase="1" duration="10m">
            <users maxnumber="1000" interarrival="5" unit="second" />
        </arrivalphase>
    </load>
    <sessions>
        <session probability="100" name="example" type="ts_http">
            <request>
                <http url="/" method="GET" />
            </request>
        </session>
    </sessions>
</tsung>
```

Run the Tsung tool using:

```
tsung start -f tsung_config.xml
```

2.2 Analyzing Tsung Results

After the test is run, Tsung generates detailed reports available in HTML format. These reports provide graphs and statistics on response times, throughput, and system performance. Access them using:

```
tsung_stats.pl --stats_dir=~/.tsung/log/$(date +%Y%m%d-%H%M)/ > report.html
```

Open the report.html file in a web browser to analyze the results.

3. Performance Testing Techniques

Apart from load testing, it is essential to measure the performance of specific system components. Here are typical performance testing techniques used in Erlang:

3.1 Micro-benchmarking

Micro-benchmarking involves testing individual functions or processes to measure the time taken for specific operations. This can be achieved using the timer:tc/3 function in Erlang:

```
-module(perf_test).
-export([test/0]).

test() ->
    {Time, Result} = timer:tc(fun() -> your_function() end),
    io:format("Execution time: ~p microseconds~nResult: ~p~n", [Time, Result]).
```

3.2 Profiling

Profiling provides a detailed analysis of function calls, execution times, and resource usage. The fprof module in Erlang is a powerful tool for profiling. Start by tracing the execution:

```
fprof:apply(fun_to_profile, []).

%% Start profiling
fprof:trace([start, {procs, all}]).

%% Execute the function you want to profile
your_function().

%% Stop profiling
fprof:trace(stop).

%% Analyze results
fprof:profile().

%% Print results to a file
fprof:analyse([{dest, "profile.txt"}]).
```

Review the profile.txt file to understand which functions consume the most resources and optimize accordingly.

3.3 Load Generation with Erlang

Erlang's concurrency model makes it well-suited for creating custom load generators. Here's an example illustrating how to generate a load using multiple processes:

```
-module(load_gen).
-export([start/1, worker/1]).

start(Num) ->
    Pids = [spawn(?MODULE, worker, [I]) || I <- lists:seq(1, Num)],
    [receive done -> ok end || _ <- lists:seq(1, Num)].

worker(Id) ->
    %% Simulate work by sleeping for random time
    timer:sleep(random:uniform(1000)),
    io:format("Worker ~p done~n", [Id]),
    %% Notify completion
    self() ! done.
```

Execute load_gen:start(100) to simulate 100 concurrent processes performing tasks.

These practices and tools enable developers to systematically measure, understand, and optimize their Erlang applications for high performance and reliability.

9.6 Debugging Tools and Techniques

Understanding and utilizing debugging tools and techniques are crucial skills for any Erlang developer. This section delves into various methods and tools available for debugging in Erlang, ensuring that developers can identify and resolve errors effectively.

The Erlang Shell: The Erlang shell is a highly interactive command-line tool that serves as a primary interface for testing and debugging Erlang code. It allows the execution of arbitrary Erlang expressions, inspection of variables, and evaluation of functions in real time. For example, to start the shell, you would execute the following command in your terminal:

```
$ erl
Erlang/OTP 24 [erts-11.2] [source] [64-bit] [smp:4:4] [ds:4:4:10] [async-threads:1] [hipe]

Eshell V11.2 (abort with ^G)
1>
```

Within the Erlang shell, you can compile and run modules, inspect variables, and even set breakpoints for detailed inspection.

Debugger: The built-in GUI debugger offers a more sophisticated way to probe into running Erlang processes. This tool supports setting breakpoints, stepping through code line-by-line, and inspecting the state of program variables. To invoke the debugger, follow these steps:

```
1> debugger:start().
```

This command will open the debugger window. From here, you can load modules that you want to be debugged using the debugged module's name. The following command loads the module my_module:

```
2> int:i(my_module).
```

Tracing: Tracing is a powerful technique for debugging concurrent systems. Erlang's tracing capabilities are provided by tools such as dbg, which allows tracing events like message passing, process creation, and function calls. Here is an example of using dbg to trace function calls in a module:

```
3> dbg:tracer().
4> dbg:p(all, c).
5> dbg:tpl(my_module, '_', []). % Trace all functions in my_module
6> dbg:tpl(io, format, x). % Specifically trace io:format/2 calls
```

```
% This will display trace outputs in the console each time "my_module" functions are called,
% or when "io:format/2" is executed.
```

Redbug: For lightweight and less intrusive tracing, Redbug is a robust option. It is particularly useful in production environments since it impacts the system performance minimally. To trace a module with Redbug, you would use the following command:

```
7> redbug:start("my_module:function/arity").
```

Redbug allows you to define specific points of interest without the overhead of the dbg tracer.

Erlang Observer: The Erlang Observer is a graphical tool that provides insights into the behavior of an Erlang application. It can monitor system metrics, load statistics, memory usage, and process information. Start the observer using:

```
8> observer:start().
```

With Observer, you can drill down into process details, memory allocation, and even visualize the supervisory tree structure of your application.

gdb with Erlang: For low-level debugging, using gdb (GNU Debugger) with Erlang can be beneficial. This is more intricate but invaluable for diagnosing crashes due to native code errors or intricate bugs in the Erlang runtime system. Compile Erlang with debug symbols to enable gdb support:

```
$ ./configure --with-dynamic-trace=dtrace
$ make
```

After compiling, start the Erlang VM with gdb:

```
$ gdb --args erl
(gdb) run
```

Once running, you can set breakpoints, inspect memory, and step through the code more thoroughly.

Process Overview and Tools: An important aspect of debugging in Erlang involves understanding process dynamics. Erlang provides several functions to query and interact with processes:

- process_info/1,2: Retrieve information about a process. - erlang:trace/3: Trace specific events in a process. - erlang:system_-flag/2: Adjust system-wide flags like back_trace.

Using these tools, developers can tightly control process behavior and gather diagnostic information.

Eper: The Eper (Erlang Performance Enhancer) suite includes multiple tools for monitoring and debugging, including etop, redbug, and exometer. These tools help in visualizing system load, process activities, and performance metrics.

To summarize, mastering these debugging tools and techniques ensures that developers can systematically approach errors in their Erlang applications, leading to more robust and efficient systems.

9.7 Using the Erlang Observer

The Erlang Observer is a powerful tool for monitoring and debugging live systems. It provides a graphical interface for observing the state of an Erlang node, making it indispensable for performance tuning, identifying bottlenecks, and diagnosing issues in running systems. This section covers the key features of the Observer, how to use it effectively, and essential tips for leveraging its capabilities.

Starting the Observer

To start the Observer GUI, initiate an Erlang shell and execute the following command:

```
observer:start().
```

Upon invocation, a window will appear displaying various tabs such as System, Load Charts, Applications, Processes, Table Viewer, and Trace Overview. Each tab offers distinct functionalities for monitoring and diagnosing the system.

System Tab

The System tab provides a holistic view of the node, offering details about memory usage, CPU utilization, run-time system information, and versions of the Erlang runtime system (ERTS) and compiler. It enables real-time monitoring of memory usage segmented into total memory, processes memory, system memory, and atom memory.

Example:

Memory Usage Display (Typical Output):

```
Total memory: 83 MB
Processes memory: 41 MB
System memory: 42 MB
Atom memory: 0.8 MB
```

Load Charts Tab

The Load Charts tab presents a visualization of the system's performance over time. It includes charts for CPU load, run queue lengths, and active processes. The data plotted in this tab help in understanding system load patterns and identifying times of high stress or underutilization.

Applications Tab

The Applications tab lists all the running applications within the node. For each application, it provides details such as the application name, version, start script, and current state. This tab facilitates the examination of the interdependencies and status of applications, which is vital for diagnosing startup issues or shutdown problems.

Processes Tab

The Processes tab is crucial for detailed process monitoring. It lists all the processes running on the node along with metadata such as the process identifier (PID), registered name, memory usage, message queue length, and current status. This table supports filters and sorts, making it easier to locate processes of interest.

Example:

```
PID Name Memory MsgQ Status
<0.50.0> my_process 1024 KB 0 waiting
<0.51.0> another_proc 512 KB 2 running
```

Clicking on a process reveals detailed information including its current call stack, message queue contents, initial call, and links to other processes. This level of detail is indispensable for diagnosing stuck processes or deadlocks.

Table Viewer Tab

The Table Viewer tab is used for inspecting the contents of ETS (Erlang Term Storage) tables. ETS tables are used for storing large amounts of data that need to be accessed concurrently by multiple processes. This tab allows you to view and filter the contents of ETS tables, making it easier to inspect what data is stored and debug issues related to data storage and retrieval.

Example:

Inspecting an ETS Table:

```
Table Name: users_table
Key        Value
1          {user, "Alice", online}
2          {user, "Bob", offline}
```

Trace Overview Tab

The Trace Overview tab offers functionality to set up and manage trace patterns. Tracing is a critical debug tool used to monitor function calls, message passing, and process activities in a live system. This tab assists in defining trace patterns, activating or deactivating them, and viewing collected trace data.

Example:

```
dbg:tracer().
dbg:p(all, [call, return_to, send, receive]).
dbg:tpl(Module, Function, arity, [{'_', [], [{return_trace}]}]).
```

This setup will trace all calls, returns, sends, and receives. The trace data would then be displayed within the Trace Overview tab, offering insights into the runtime behavior of the system.

Tips for Effective Use of Observer

- Regularly monitor the System and Load Charts tabs to spot performance degradations early.
- Use the Processes tab to identify processes with growing message queues, which could indicate bottlenecks.
- Utilize the Applications tab to ensure that all expected applications are running and in the correct state.
- Leverage the Table Viewer tab to validate data consistency in ETS tables.
- Implement selective tracing via the Trace Overview tab to minimize performance overhead while capturing relevant debug information.

By integrating the Erlang Observer into your monitoring and debugging routines, you can gain valuable visibility into the live state of your system, facilitating quicker and more accurate issue resolution.

9.8 Profiling and Optimization

Profiling and optimization are critical activities that help improve the performance and efficiency of Erlang applications. Profiling involves collecting data to identify bottlenecks, while optimization focuses on refining code to enhance performance. This section delves into various profiling tools and techniques available in Erlang and best practices for optimizing code.

Erlang provides several tools to profile applications, such as fprof, eprof, cprof, and Percept. Each of these tools serves a specific purpose and offers unique benefits. Below is an overview of these profiling tools.

fprof is a profiling tool that offers detailed analysis of function calls within an Erlang application. To use fprof, the following steps are typically followed:

```
% Start profiling
fprof:apply(Module, Function, Args).

% Analyze the generated profile data
fprof:profile(FileName).

% Read and display the analysis results
fprof:analyse(FileName).
```

% Output example: detailed function call information with execution times

The apply/3 function initiates profiling, and an analysis file is generated. The profile/1 function processes this data, while analyse/1 displays the results.

eprof focuses on time analysis specifically related to how much time is spent in each Erlang process. Using eprof involves the following steps:

```
% Start tracing
eprof:start().

% Profile a specific process
eprof:start_profiling(Process).

% Execute the code to be profiled
... % code execution

% Stop profiling
eprof:stop_profiling().

% Analyze collected profile data
eprof:analyze().
```

% Output example: time spent in each process

Similarly, cprof provides a straightforward way to understand how many times each function is called in the system. This is useful when understanding the usage patterns of functions within the application.

```
% Start profiling
cprof:start().

% Profile a specific function call
cprof:tpl(Module, Function, Arity).

% Execute the code
... % code execution

% Stop profiling
cprof:stop().

% Display profile results
cprof:analyze(Module, Function, Arity).
```

% Output example: number of calls per function

Another vital profiling tool is Percept, focusing on concurrency profiling. Percept provides insight into the behavior of concurrent processes to help diagnose concurrency issues and optimize concurrent performance. The usage involves:

```
% Start Percept profiling
percept:start().

% Run your code
... % code execution

% Stop Percept profiling
percept:stop().

% Analyze the profiling results
percept:profile_text(start_date, end_date).
```

% Output example: visualized concurrency profiling with graphical representation

Having covered profiling tools, we now turn to optimization techniques. Here are some key practices:

- **Avoid Overloading Processes:** Ensuring that no single process is overloaded is vital. Distribute workload efficiently to prevent bottlenecks. Sharding techniques may be applied when necessary.
- **Optimize Recursion:** Use tail recursion where possible to reduce stack usage. Tail recursion enables more efficient memory utilization.
- **Minimize Message Passing:** Excessive message passing between processes can lead to congestion. Group related opera-

tions together where feasible.

- **Utilize Efficient Data Structures:** Select appropriate data structures, such as ets tables, based on usage patterns. Processing efficiency depends heavily on the choice of data representation.

For example, consider the following optimizable recursive function:

```
% Non-tail recursive version
sum([H|T]) -> H + sum(T);
sum([]) -> 0.
```

This can be optimized using tail recursion:

```
% Tail recursive version
sum(List) -> sum(List, 0).

sum([H|T], Acc) -> sum(T, Acc + H);
sum([], Acc) -> Acc.
```

% Output example: optimized tail recursive sum function

These optimizations should be tested to verify improvements. Benchmarks provide a means to compare performance before and after changes. Utilizing benchmarking tools like basho_bench allows for detailed performance analysis under various workloads:

```
% Sample basho_bench config file
[
  {driver, basho_bench_driver,
    [
      {code_path, "ebin"},
      {modules, [example]}]}
].
```

% Output example: detailed benchmarking results

Profiling tools and optimization techniques are indispensable for maintaining efficient Erlang applications. Applying these strategies ensures that an application scales and performs efficiently under growing demands.

Chapter 10

Advanced Topics

This chapter delves into advanced topics in Erlang, covering metaprogramming with macros, distributed systems, and interfacing with other languages. It addresses hot code upgrades, advanced optimization techniques, and Erlang in cloud computing. The chapter also explores security best practices and examines emerging trends and future directions in the Erlang ecosystem.

10.1 Introduction to Advanced Erlang

Erlang's powerful features and abstractions equip programmers to handle a myriad of complex problems, especially in concurrent and distributed systems. Advanced topics in Erlang build upon the foundational principles introduced in earlier chapters, ensuring the efficient and robust handling of real-world scenarios. This section explores sophisticated techniques and methodologies that seasoned Erlang developers utilize to leverage the language's full potential.

Erlang's concurrency model, based on lightweight processes, is fundamental in understanding advanced applications. Each Erlang process is isolated, communicating with others via message passing, ensuring that failure in one part of the system doesn't cascade to others. This fault-tolerant architecture is intrinsic in designing resilient systems and sets a strong foundation for advanced concepts.

Actor Model: The primary paradigm underlying Erlang's concurrency model is the Actor model. In this model, actors are the universal primitives that:

- Encapsulate state and behavior.
- Communicate exclusively through asynchronous message passing.
- Make local decisions and generate responses.

Erlang's handling of the Actor model ensures that processes do not share memory, minimizing errors stemming from race conditions and shared-state concurrency issues. The following example illustrates the creation and interaction of Erlang processes:

```
-module(actor_example).
-export([start/0, actor/0]).
start() ->
    Pid = spawn(?MODULE, actor, []),
    Pid ! {hello, self()},
    receive
        {hello_reply, Msg} -> io:format("Received: ~p~n", [Msg])
    end.

actor() ->
    receive
        {hello, From} ->
            From ! {hello_reply, "Hello back!"},
            actor()
    end.
```

In this example, the start/0 function spawns a new process to run the actor/0 function. The spawned process receives a message and replies, showcasing the elementary mechanics of Erlang's messaging system.

Supervision Trees: Erlang introduces the concept of supervision trees to manage process lifecycles and recovery. Supervisors are responsible for starting, stopping, and monitoring their child processes, which may include other supervisors or workers. This hierarchical arrangement allows for the systematic recovery of failed processes:

```
-module(supervisor_example).
-behaviour(supervisor).

-export([start_link/0, init/1]).

start_link() ->
    supervisor:start_link({local, ?MODULE}, ?MODULE, []).

init([]) ->
    {ok, {{one_for_one, 5, 10}, [
```

```
    {child, {worker, worker_example, []}, permanent, brutal_kill, worker, [
          worker_example]}
  ]}}.
```

The supervisor_example module demonstrates the definition of a basic supervisor. The init/1 function specifies the supervision strategy, one_for_one, where each child process is treated independently; if it terminates, only that particular process is restarted. The configuration includes restart intensity (5 restarts in 10 seconds), ensuring system stability under varying failure scenarios.

Error Handling and Fault Tolerance: Erlang's error handling philosophy, often summarized as "let it crash," delegates error management to supervisory structures. By allowing processes to fail and be restarted by their supervisors, the system maintains overall stability and minimizes complex error handling logic within individual processes.

```
-module(worker_example).
-export([start_link/0, init/1, handle_call/3, handle_cast/2, terminate/2]).

start_link() ->
    gen_server:start_link({local, ?MODULE}, ?MODULE, [], []).

init([]) ->
    {ok, #state{}}.

handle_call({do_work, Data}, _From, State) ->
    Result = perform_task(Data),
    {reply, Result, State}.

handle_cast({update, NewData}, State) ->
    {noreply, NewState} = update_state(NewData, State),
    {noreply, NewState}.

terminate(_Reason, _State) ->
    ok.
```

In the worker_example module, a generic server (gen_server) is used to handle synchronous (handle_call/3) and asynchronous (handle_-cast/2) messages. If the server encounters a critical error, it is terminated and restarted by its supervisor, preserving the system's operational integrity.

Hot Code Upgrades: One of Erlang's distinguishing features is its support for hot code upgrades. This allows for code changes to be applied without stopping the system, ensuring continuous availability. The hot code loading mechanism typically involves the following steps:

- Load the new version of the module using l(Module).
- Transition processes to use the new code version through specific

upgrade instructions in the code_change callback for gen_server, gen_fsm, or gen_statem behaviors.

```
-module(hot_upgrade_example).
-behaviour(gen_server).

-export([start_link/0, init/1, code_change/3, handle_call/3]).

start_link() ->
    gen_server:start_link({local, ?MODULE}, ?MODULE, [], []).

init([]) ->
    {ok, #state{}}.

handle_call({upgrade_me}, _From, State) ->
    {reply, "Upgraded", State}.

code_change(_OldVsn, State, _Extra) ->
    {ok, State}.
```

The code_change/3 function facilitates the state migration during a code upgrade, allowing for an uninterrupted service.

Understanding these advanced aspects of Erlang is crucial for designing systems that are not only resilient and fault-tolerant but also maintainable and efficient. The following sections will dive deeper into specific advanced topics, building on these foundational concepts.

10.2 Metaprogramming with Macros

Metaprogramming in Erlang, particularly through the use of macros, allows developers to introduce a higher level of abstraction and flexibility in program code. Macros in Erlang are defined using the preprocessor and can be used to substitute code patterns, making them powerful tools for code reuse and conditional compilation.

Erlang macros are defined using the -define directive, which has the following general form:

```
-define(MACRO_NAME, ReplacementText).
```

Here, MACRO_NAME is an identifier, and ReplacementText is the code snippet or value that the macro will expand into wherever it is invoked in the code. When the Erlang preprocessor encounters ?MACRO_NAME, it replaces it with ReplacementText.

For instance, consider the following simple macro:

```
-define(PI, 3.14159).
```

Whenever ?PI is used in the code, it will be replaced with 3.14159. Such macros are straightforward and can help eliminate magic numbers, thereby enhancing code readability.

A more advanced use case involves parameterized macros, which accept arguments and allow for greater flexibility in the substitution process. The definition syntax for parameterized macros is as follows:

```
-define(MACRO_NAME(Arg1, Arg2, ...), ReplacementText).
```

When invoking a parameterized macro, you provide the necessary arguments, and the preprocessor replaces the macro invocation with the ReplacementText, substituting the provided arguments. As an example, consider a macro that calculates the area of a circle:

```
-define(CIRCLE_AREA(Radius), ?PI * (Radius) * (Radius)).
```

This macro can be used in the code as follows:

```
Area = ?CIRCLE_AREA(10).
```

The preprocessor will replace the above line with:

```
Area = 3.14159 * (10) * (10).
```

Macros can also be employed for conditional compilation, aiding in the development process by including or excluding code depending on certain conditions. This capability is particularly useful for platform-specific code or debugging purposes. Conditional compilation in Erlang is achieved using the -ifdef, -ifndef, -else, and -endif directives. Here is an example demonstrating these directives:

```
-define(DEBUG, true).

-module(example).

-ifdef(DEBUG).
-define(LOG(Expr), io:format("Debug: ~p~n", [Expr])).
-else.
-define(LOG(Expr), ok).
-endif.

foo() ->
    ?LOG("This is a debug log message").
```

In this case, if the DEBUG macro is defined, the LOG macro will be replaced by io:format("Debug: p n", [Expr]). Otherwise, it will be replaced by ok. This allows you to enable or disable debug logging easily.

Metaprogramming with macros in Erlang provides a vital toolset for more expressive and maintainable code. By allowing patterns and boilerplates to be encapsulated, macros can reduce redundancy and potential errors in large codebases. When used judiciously, they contribute significantly to making the code both efficient and clean. Developers should, however, take caution not to overuse macros, as excessive complexity in replacement definitions can lead to code that is difficult to follow and debug.

It is also important to remember that macros are purely a textual replacement mechanism and operate before the actual compilation phase. Thus, syntax errors resulting from macro expansions will occur during preprocessing, complicating debugging. As a best practice, macros should be kept simple, intuitive, and well-documented to maintain code clarity and facilitate easier maintenance.

In addition, the module attributes and other preprocessor directives embedded in macros should adhere to the module's naming conventions and coding standards. Appropriate commenting around macro definitions can help future developers understand their purpose and usage context, reducing the cognitive load during code reviews and subsequent modifications.

10.3 Distributed Erlang Systems

Distributed systems are a foundational aspect of Erlang's design philosophy. Erlang was built with distribution in mind, aiming to provide out-of-the-box support for building scalable and fault-tolerant systems. This section will cover the core aspects of distributed Erlang systems, including node creation and communication, process distribution, failure detection, and strategies for scaling and maintaining such systems.

Node Creation and Communication

In Erlang, a node is an instance of the Erlang runtime system capable of communicating with other nodes. Each node is identified by a name of the format Name@Host, where Name is an atom and Host is either an IP address or a hostname. To start a node, the -sname or -name command line flag is used:

```
$ erl -sname mynode
```

This command starts an Erlang shell with the node name mynode on the local host. For communication between nodes, it is essential to ensure they're aware of each other. Nodes can connect using the net_adm:ping/1 function:

```
net_adm:ping('anothernode@hostname').
```

If the function returns pong, the nodes are successfully connected. One node can send a message to a process on another node using the standard message passing syntax:

```
Pid ! Message.
```

Where Pid is the process identifier, which can be a local process or a remote one using the format {Pid, Node}.

Process Distribution

Erlang's spawn/1, spawn/3, and spawn_link/3 functions support process creation on remote nodes. For instance, spawning a process on a specific node is achieved through:

```
spawn('targetnode@hostname', Module, Function, Args).
```

This command will create a new process on targetnode@hostname that evaluates Module:Function(Args).

Failure Detection and Handling

Erlang's robust failure detection mechanism leverages the monitor/2 and link/1 functions. When a process monitors another process, it receives a DOWN message if the monitored process terminates. Linking two processes results in a bidirectional relationship where either process receives an EXIT signal if the other terminates:

```
Pid = spawn_link('remote@node', Module, Function, Args),
exit(Pid, Reason).
```

Inserting these constructs ensures that failures are not silent and can be acted upon by supervising processes.

Scalability Strategies

Scaling distributed Erlang systems involves both horizontal and vertical scaling mechanisms. Horizontal scaling through clustering involves adding more nodes to the distributed system, whereas vertical scaling addresses enhancing individual node capacity.

Erlang/OTP provides the global module to manage global names across the nodes, ensuring that processes can be located and invoked irrespective of their physical location:

```
global:register_name(Name, Pid),
global:whereis_name(Name).
```

To further enhance distribution, the pg2 module enables process grouping, allowing processes to be grouped logically:

```
pg2:create(Group),
pg2:join(Group, Pid),
pg2:get_members(Group).
```

Maintaining System Health

Regularly monitoring system health is crucial when dealing with distributed systems. Tools such as observer and the sys_sup behavior facilitate real-time monitoring and system health checks. The observer application provides a graphical interface to inspect processes, load, and communication between nodes:

```
observer:start().
```

Designing distributed systems also necessitates considering network partitioning and data consistency strategies. Using algorithms like two-phase commit (2PC) or paxos ensures that the system remains consistent despite node failures or network issues.

Algorithm 2: Two-Phase Commit Protocol

```
Data: Participants, Coordinator
Result: Transaction Commit or Abort
foreach Participant in Participants do
    Participant ← prepare ;
    if prepare fails then
        abort transaction and notify the coordinator;
        exit;
if all participants prepared successfully then
    foreach Participant in Participants do
        commit transaction ;
else
    foreach Participant in Participants do
        abort transaction;
```

Deploying a distributed system also requires implementing a consistent monitoring approach, maintaining logs, performing regular audits, and guaranteeing sufficient redundancy and backups to handle unexpected failures efficiently.

10.4 Interfacing with Other Languages

Interfacing with other programming languages enhances the capabilities of Erlang systems by leveraging existing libraries and functionalities written in those languages. This section explores various strategies for integrating Erlang with C, C++, Java, and Python, providing concrete examples and detailed explanations.

Natively Implemented Functions (NIFs)

Natively Implemented Functions (NIFs) allow Erlang to execute functions written in C or C++. NIFs are useful for performance-critical parts of an application but must be used with caution due to potential risks such as crashes or deadlocks.

Firstly, we must create a C file for our NIFs. Consider the following C code:

```
#include "erl_nif.h"

static ERL_NIF_TERM add(ErlNifEnv* env, int argc, const ERL_NIF_TERM argv
    []) {
    int a, b;
    if (!enif_get_int(env, argv[0], &a) || !enif_get_int(env, argv[1], &b)) {
        return enif_make_badarg(env);
    }
    return enif_make_int(env, a + b);
}

static ErlNifFunc nif_funcs[] = {
    {"add", 2, add}
};

ERL_NIF_INIT(my_nif, nif_funcs, NULL, NULL, NULL, NULL)
```

Compile the C code to a shared object library.

```
gcc -o my_nif.so -shared -fPIC my_nif.c
```

In the Erlang module, we need to load the shared library and define the interface to the NIF:

```
-module(my_nif).
-export([add/2, load_nif/0]).

load_nif() ->
```

```
    erlang:load_nif("./my_nif", 0).

add(_A, _B) ->
    erlang:nif_error("NIF library not loaded").
```

After loading the NIF library with my_nif:load_nif/0, the add/2 function will execute the corresponding C code, offering a substantial performance improvement for computationally intensive tasks.

Erlang Ports

Erlang Ports provide a mechanism to communicate with external programs written in any language. This method uses standard input/output for data exchange.

Here is an example using a simple Python script:

Create the Python script:

```
import sys

for line in sys.stdin:
    try:
        a, b = map(int, line.strip().split())
        print(a + b)
    except Exception as e:
        print("error:", e)
```

Create the Erlang module to interact with the Python script:

```
-module(port_example).
-export([start/0, add/2]).

start() ->
    Port = open_port({spawn, "python3 add.py"}, [{line, 1024},{packet, 2}]),
    loop(Port).

loop(Port) ->
    receive
        {data, Data} ->
            io:format("Received: ~s~n", [Data]),
            loop(Port);
        {add, A, B} ->
            Port ! {self(), {command, lists:concat([integer_to_list(A), " ",
                      integer_to_list(B), "\n"])}},
            loop(Port)
    end.

add(Pid, A, B) ->
    Pid ! {add, A, B}.
```

To interact with the Python script, compile and run the Erlang code.

```
1> c(port_example).
2> Pid = port_example:start().
3> port_example:add(Pid, 3, 5).
```

You will see the output from the Python script being displayed on the Erlang shell. This ensures that the additional computation is offloaded to an external program while maintaining robust communication.

Java Interoperability with JInterface

JInterface is a library provided by the Erlang/OTP distribution that allows communication between Erlang and Java. To demonstrate, we need to set up a Java project with JInterface dependency.

Define a Java class for interaction:

```
import com.ericsson.otp.erlang.*;

public class JavaServer {
    public static void main(String[] args) {
        OtpNode node = new OtpNode("javanode@localhost", "secretcookie");
        OtpMbox mbox = node.createMbox("javaServer");

        while (true) {
            try {
                OtpErlangObject obj = mbox.receive();
                OtpErlangTuple msg = (OtpErlangTuple) obj;
                OtpErlangPid from = (OtpErlangPid) msg.elementAt(0);
                OtpErlangInt ei1 = (OtpErlangInt) msg.elementAt(1);
                OtpErlangInt ei2 = (OtpErlangInt) msg.elementAt(2);

                int sum = ei1.intValue() + ei2.intValue();
                mbox.send(from, new OtpErlangInt(sum));
            } catch (Exception e) {
                e.printStackTrace();
            }
        }
    }
}
```

Configure the Erlang module to communicate with the Java node:

```
-module(erlang_to_java).
-export([start/0, add/2]).

start() ->
    net_adm:ping('javanode@localhost').

add(A, B) ->
    self() ! {self(), A, B},
    mbox_example:send('javaServer@localhost', {self(), A, B}).
```

In this integration, Erlang sends messages to a Java node which then processes and returns the result. This setup permits the use of Java libraries and frameworks effectively.

Python with Erlport

Erlport provides a straightforward way to interface Python and Erlang. First, of course, install Erlport in your Python environment.

The Python code utilizing Erlport:

```
from erlport.erlterms import Atom
from erlport.erlang import set_message_handler, cast, call

def add(a, b):
    return a + b

if __name__ == "__main__":
    set_message_handler(add)
```

Then, create and run the corresponding Erlang module:

```
-module(erlang_python).
-export([start/0, add/2]).

start() ->
    Port = open_port({spawn, "python3 add.py"}, [{packet, 2}]).

add(A, B) ->
    Port = erlang_python:start(),
    Port ! {self(), {call, add, [A, B]}},
    receive
        {Port, {call, add, [Result]}} ->
            io:format("Result: ~p~n", [Result])
    end.
```

These few approaches for interfacing Erlang with other programming languages significantly enhance the overall versatility, ensuring that developers can utilize existing tools and libraries from various technological stacks within an Erlang application.

10.5 Hot Code Upgrades

Hot code upgrades in Erlang are a powerful feature that allows you to update a running system without stopping it. This capability is essential for systems requiring high availability, where downtime must be minimized or eliminated. In this section, we will explore how hot code upgrades work, the mechanisms provided by Erlang to accomplish them, and best practices to ensure that upgrades are smooth and error-free.

Erlang's VM, BEAM, is designed to support multiple versions of a module running simultaneously. This feature allows a new version of a module to be loaded while the old version is still in use, enabling a running system to switch to the new code without disruption.

code:load_binary/3 is the primary function used to load new versions of a module dynamically. The function signature is as follows:

```
code:load_binary(Module, FileName, Binary) -> {module, Module} | error
```

Here, Module is the name of the module being upgraded, FileName is the name of the file from which the module is loaded, and Binary is the compiled beam code.

Erlang also provides a mechanism called "application upgrade," which involves more comprehensive changes, including upgrading multiple modules and state transformations. The .appup file plays a critical role in this process. This file contains instructions for upgrading and downgrading versions of the application.

An example .appup file:

```
{"1.1",
 [{"1.0", [{load_module, my_module}, {load_module, another_module}]}],

 "1.0",
 [{"1.1", [{load_module, my_module}, {load_module, another_module}]}]
}.
```

In the above file, the version "1.1" includes upgrade instructions from "1.0" to "1.1," and downgrade instructions from "1.1" to "1.0." The tuple {load_module, my_module} specifies which modules to load during the upgrade.

When performing hot code upgrades, special attention must be given to the transformation of state between versions. Erlang provides the following mechanisms to handle state changes:

- The code_change/3 callback function in the gen_server behaviour module is used to convert the state when a new version of the module is loaded.
- This function has the following signature:

```
Module:code_change(OldVsn, State, Extra) -> {ok, NewState}
```

OldVsn represents the old version of the state, State is the current state, and Extra contains any additional data needed for the conversion.

```
code_change(OldVsn, State, Extra) ->
    NewState = state_transform(State),
    {ok, NewState}.
```

In this example, state_transform/1 is a hypothetical function designed to convert the old state to the new state format.

The upgrade process also needs to handle possible synchronization issues between processes, given that messages in transit may rely on the old state structure. Best practices include:

- Ensuring that the new code is backward compatible, whenever possible, to handle messages expected by the old code.
- Using version tags within state data structures can help manage changes over time.
- Thorough testing in a staging environment that mimics the production environment can help identify issues before the upgrade is applied.
- When multiple nodes are involved (in a distributed system), a coordinated upgrade strategy to avoid inconsistencies.

To manage these upgrades programmatically and in a structured manner, you can use Erlang's release_handler module, which is part of the OTP applications. This module offers functions like release_upgrade/1 to facilitate upgrades:

```
release_handler:install_release("1.1").
```

Using release_handler helps in managing the complexity associated with rolling back changes in case of an upgrade failure. By encapsulating these processes within versioned releases managed by OTP, you achieve more reliable and maintainable upgrades.

One common challenge experienced during hot code upgrades is managing changes in external dependencies. It's essential to account for any differences in API or behavior of these dependencies between versions, ensuring that the new code adheres to the required interface contracts.

Implementing hot code upgrades effectively requires careful planning and designing your system to accommodate state transformations, backward compatibility, and proper testing. The tools provided by Erlang, such as code_change/3 and release_handler, facilitate the process but should be used with strategic foresight. Advanced monitoring and logging practices also help in immediately identifying and addressing issues post-upgrade, maintaining the high availability of your application.

10.6 Advanced Optimization Techniques

Erlang, known for its concurrency model and fault-tolerant behavior, offers various optimization techniques to enhance performance. These techniques encompass both code-level optimizations and system-level configurations. This section discusses advanced strategies that leverage the intricacies of the Erlang runtime system (ERTS) and the nuances of the language itself.

Code-Level Optimizations

One fundamental approach to optimization in Erlang involves streamlining the code execution paths and minimizing unnecessary computations. Pattern matching, tail call optimization, and efficient data structures play crucial roles in this regard.

Pattern matching, a core feature of Erlang, allows for clear and concise code but can introduce inefficiencies if not utilized wisely. When pattern matching, it is essential to order patterns from most specific to most general to reduce the number of comparisons. For instance, when matching against multiple tuples, place the more specific patterns first:

```
% Inefficient pattern order
case Tuple of
    {_, _} -> % general case
        % do something
    {a, b} -> % specific case
        % do something specific
end.

% Efficient pattern order
case Tuple of
    {a, b} -> % specific case
        % do something specific
    {_, _} -> % general case
        % do something
end.
```

Tail call optimization (TCO) is another critical aspect. A function call is in a tail position if it is the last action in the function. Erlang's runtime system can optimize tail calls to prevent stack growth, which is crucial for recursion-heavy algorithms. Ensuring that recursive calls are the last operation in a function can make a significant difference:

```
% Non-tail recursive function
factorial(N) ->
    N * factorial(N - 1).

% Tail recursive function
factorial(N) ->
    factorial(N, 1).
```

```
factorial(0, Acc) -> Acc;
factorial(N, Acc) -> factorial(N - 1, N * Acc).
```

Using appropriate data structures is also vital. For example, lists are suitable for small to medium-sized collections due to their dynamic nature and simplicity in pattern matching. For larger datasets where frequent updates are needed, tuples or maps may offer better performance. Understanding the O(1) and O(n) characteristics of these data structures aids in making informed decisions.

ETS Tables and Mnesia

Erlang Term Storage (ETS) and Mnesia are two built-in databases providing efficient data storage capabilities. ETS tables are an excellent choice for in-memory storage, supporting concurrent reads and writes, and are suitable for high-performance applications needing rapid access to data:

```
% Creating an ETS table
Table = ets:new(my_table, [named_table, public, set]).

% Inserting data into ETS
ets:insert(my_table, {key, value}).

% Retrieving data from ETS
case ets:lookup(my_table, key) of
    [] -> none;
    [{_, Value}] -> Value
end.
```

Mnesia, on the other hand, is a distributed database management system (DBMS) built on top of ETS. It supports transactions, which make it suitable for applications requiring strong consistency guarantees:

```
% Creating a Mnesia schema
mnesia:create_schema([node()]).
mnesia:start().

% Defining a table in Mnesia
TableDef = {my_table, [{attributes, record_info(fields, my_table)}]}.
mnesia:create_table(my_table, TableDef).

% Performing transactions in Mnesia
mnesia:transaction(fun() ->
    mnesia:write(#my_table{key = key, value = value})
end).

mnesia:transaction(fun() ->
    case mnesia:read({my_table, key}) of
        [] -> none;
        [Record] -> Record#my_table.value
    end
end).
```

Concurrency Optimization

Optimizing the concurrency model involves efficient process management and load distribution. Erlang's lightweight processes allow for massive concurrency, but proper usage is critical to achieving optimal performance.

Using process pools can help manage resources effectively by reusing processes for repetitive tasks, reducing the overhead of continually spawning and terminating processes:

```
% Implementing a simple process pool
start_pool(Size) ->
    Pool = lists:map(fun(_) -> spawn(fun worker/0) end, lists:seq(1, Size)),
    {ok, Pool}.

worker() ->
    receive
        {work, Task} ->
            Task(),
            worker() % loop to wait for the next task
    end.
```

Load distribution can be improved by using the pg2 module for managing and balancing across process groups, ensuring that tasks are evenly distributed among available workers:

```
% Using pg2 for load balancing
pg2:create(my_group),
pg2:join(my_group, self()).

% Broadcasting tasks to all members
pg2:get_members(my_group) ! {work, MyTask}.
```

System-Level Optimizations

System-level optimizations involve tweaking the Erlang VM (BEAM) settings and the underlying OS configurations. For instance, configuring the number of scheduler threads can impact how well the VM utilizes CPU resources. Use the +S flag to set the number of schedulers:

```
% Starting the Erlang VM with 4 scheduler threads
erl +S 4
```

Additionally, understanding and utilizing dirty schedulers for tasks involving blocking operations can relieve the default scheduler threads, thus maintaining responsiveness in the system. Enabling dirty schedulers can be done via the application's configuration:

```
% Enabling dirty schedulers
erl +sbt db
```

Fine-tuning the garbage collection (GC) process is another optimization area. Adjusting the garbage collection strategy using the +hms and +hmb flags can benefit memory-intensive applications:

```
% Setting heap sizes for minimal and maximum heap blocks allocation
erl +hms 512 +hmb 1024
```

The interconnectivity of code and system optimization techniques in Erlang, when applied judiciously, can lead to substantial performance improvements, making the system more efficient and responsive.

10.7 Erlang and Cloud Computing

Erlang's inherent design makes it an excellent choice for cloud computing. Its ability to handle massive numbers of concurrent processes, fault tolerance, and distribution capabilities align well with the demands of cloud environments. This section explores key concepts and practices, demonstrating how Erlang is utilized in cloud computing, including deployment strategies, scaling techniques, and integrating with cloud service providers.

One of Erlang's core strengths lies in its lightweight processes and efficient message-passing capabilities. When deploying Erlang applications in the cloud, these characteristics support scalability and robustness. A common approach to cloud deployment involves containerization using Docker. Containers encapsulate the application with its dependencies, ensuring consistent execution across different environments. Below, we see an example Dockerfile for an Erlang application.

```
# Use the official Erlang base image
FROM erlang:latest

# Set the working directory
WORKDIR /app

# Copy the project files
COPY . /app

# Compile the application
RUN rebar3 compile

# Specify the command to run the application
CMD ["rebar3", "shell"]
```

In this Dockerfile, the base image is set to erlang:latest, and the working directory is defined as /app. The application files are copied into the container, and rebar3 compile is executed to compile the application.

Finally, the container launches the Erlang shell.

Scalability in cloud computing corresponds to adjusting resources in response to demand. Erlang's architecture supports simple horizontal scaling, i.e., adding more nodes to the system. In a cloud environment, we can automate the scaling process using orchestration tools such as Kubernetes. Kubernetes handles the management of containerized applications across a cluster of machines, ensuring that the desired state of the application is maintained. For instance, the following Kubernetes deployment script demonstrates how to deploy an Erlang application:

```
apiVersion: apps/v1
kind: Deployment
metadata:
  name: erlang-app
spec:
  replicas: 3
  selector:
    matchLabels:
      app: erlang-app
  template:
    metadata:
      labels:
        app: erlang-app
    spec:
      containers:
      - name: erlang
        image: erlang-app:latest
        ports:
        - containerPort: 8080
```

This YAML script defines a deployment of an Erlang application with three replicas. Kubernetes ensures that three instances of the application are running, distributing the load and resources as specified.

Erlang's native capabilities, such as node connectivity, are particularly advantageous in cloud computing. By using the net_adm and net_kernel modules, nodes can be dynamically connected and monitored. Below is an example demonstrating how to connect nodes in an Erlang environment:

```
% Start the Erlang shell for node1
$ erl -name node1@hostname -setcookie secret_cookie

% Start the Erlang shell for node2 and connect to node1
$ erl -name node2@hostname -setcookie secret_cookie

% In the Erlang shell of node1
(node1@hostname)1> net_adm:ping('node2@hostname').
pong
```

Using the -name flag, each node is given a unique name within the network, and -setcookie ensures secure communication. The net_-

adm:ping function enables one node to verify connectivity with another.

An aspect crucial to cloud computing is integrating with cloud service providers such as AWS, GCP, or Azure. Erlang applications can leverage these platforms for enhanced capabilities, such as storage solutions, managed databases, and load balancers. For example, integrating with Amazon S3 for storage can be achieved through the erlcloud library. The following code snippet demonstrates how to upload a file to Amazon S3:

```
% Start erlcloud application
application:ensure_all_started(erlcloud).

% Configure AWS credentials
erlcloud:config(#{access_key_id => "YOUR_ACCESS_KEY",
                 secret_access_key => "YOUR_SECRET_KEY",
                 region => "us-east-1"}).

% Upload a file to S3
erlcloud_s3:put_object("bucket-name", "new-file.txt", "file content").
```

After ensuring the erlcloud application is started and AWS credentials are configured, the erlcloud_s3:put_object function uploads a file to the specified S3 bucket.

Security is paramount in cloud computing, and Erlang provides robust mechanisms for secure communication and data protection. Establishing encrypted connections between nodes can be achieved using SSL/TLS. Here, we illustrate securing communication between two nodes:

```
% Generate SSL certificates and keys using OpenSSL
$ openssl req -newkey rsa:2048 -nodes -keyout server.key -x509 -days 365 -out server.crt

% Configure nodes to use SSL
(node1@hostname)1> ssl:start().
(node1@hostname)2> ssl:connect('node2@hostname', 636, [{keyfile, "server.key"}, {
    certfile, "server.crt"}]).
```

By generating SSL certificates and using the ssl:start and ssl:connect functions, encrypted channels between nodes are established.

To further illustrate Erlang's application in cloud computing, consider its usage in modern cloud-native architectures such as microservices. Each microservice can be an independent Erlang application communicating with others through well-defined APIs. Tools like gRPC and REST can facilitate these communications. For example, creating a simple REST API in Erlang using the cowboy HTTP server can be implemented as follows:

```
% Define router for REST API
-module(my_rest_router).
```

```
-export([init/4]).

init(Req, _Opts) ->
    {ok, Req, my_rest_handler}.

% Define request handler
-module(my_rest_handler).
-export([init/4, handle/2]).

init(Req, Opts) ->
    {ok, Req, Opts}.

handle(Req, State) ->
    {ok, Req2} = cowboy_req:reply(200, #{<<"content-type">> => <<"application/
        json">>}, <<"Hello, World!">>, Req),
    {ok, Req2, State}.

% Start cowboy server
-module(my_app).
-export([start/0, stop/0]).

start() ->
    {ok, _} = cowboy:start_clear(http_listener, [{port, 8080}], #{env => #{dispatch
        => cowboy_router:compile([{'_', [{"/", my_rest_router, []}]}])}}).

stop() ->
    ok = cowboy:stop_listener(http_listener).
```

Deploying this simple REST API service in a cloud-native environment allows for scalable, fault-tolerant applications, embodying the principles of microservices architecture.

Erlang's design is synergistic with the dynamic and distributed nature of cloud computing. Its strengths in concurrency, fault tolerance, and distributed processing empower developers to build resilient and efficient cloud-native applications. Integrating with modern cloud infrastructure and services further enhances these capabilities, providing a comprehensive toolkit for contemporary cloud computing challenges.

10.8 Security and Best Practices

In ensuring the robustness and reliability of systems built with Erlang, addressing security concerns and adhering to best practices is paramount. Security in Erlang can be approached from several angles: safeguarding the codebase, securing communication channels, managing secrets appropriately, and ensuring robust error handling.

Erlang provides several built-in mechanisms and libraries that assist in enforcing security. This section provides a detailed examination of these mechanisms and guidelines for leveraging them effectively.

1. **Codebase Security**

    - Secure Coding Standards: Adhering to secure coding standards involves writing code that is free from common vulnerabilities such as buffer overflows, race conditions, and improper access controls. Erlang, being a functional language with immutable data, inherently avoids some of these pitfalls, but diligence is necessary.

    - Code Reviews: Regular code reviews help ensure that vulnerabilities are caught early. Incorporating automated tools for static code analysis can further enhance this process.

2. **Securing Communication Channels**

    - TLS/SSL: Ensuring secure communication between Erlang nodes and external systems often involves Transport Layer Security (TLS) or Secure Sockets Layer (SSL). Erlang provides the ssl application, which can be used to create secure connections.

```
% Example of starting an SSL connection
{ok, ListenSocket} = ssl:listen(Port, [{certfile, "path/to/cert.pem"}, {keyfile,
        "path/to/key.pem"}]),
{ok, Socket} = ssl:transport_accept(ListenSocket),
ssl:ssl_accept(Socket).
```

    - Encryption and Decryption: For data that needs to be encrypted and decrypted, the crypto module is available.

```
% Example of encryption and decryption
Key = crypto:strong_rand_bytes(32),
IV = crypto:strong_rand_bytes(16),
CipherText = crypto:block_encrypt(aes_cbc, Key, IV, PlainText),
PlainText = crypto:block_decrypt(aes_cbc, Key, IV, CipherText).
```

3. **Managing Secrets**

    - Environment Variables: Storing secrets in environment variables can reduce the risk of leakage compared to hardcoding them in the source code.

    - Encrypted Storage: For persisting sensitive information, encrypting data before saving it to storage (e.g., database, file system) is advisable.

- Secret Rotation: Regularly changing secrets and keys reduces the window of opportunity for an attacker to exploit compromised keys.

4. Robust Error Handling

Robust error handling is crucial for maintaining security in a distributed system. Erlang's "let it crash" philosophy is complemented by its supervision trees, which can be designed to detect and recover from errors efficiently.

Algorithm 3: Basic Supervision Tree

```
Data: Supervisor Initialization
Result: Supervision Tree Setup
begin
    Children = [ worker, my_worker, start_link, [], permanent,
      5000, worker, [my_worker] ];
    SupervisorSpec = simple_one_for_one, 5, 3600;
    ok, one_for_one, 1, 5, Children =
    supervisor:start_link(SupervisorSpec)
```

5. Access Control

By using access control mechanisms, you can make sure that only authorized entities can interact with your Erlang nodes.

- Node Authentication: Configuring node authentication with cookies is a primary method for ensuring that only trusted nodes can communicate.

```
% Setting node cookie
os:putenv("COOKIE", "YourSecretCookie"),
net_adm:ping('other@node'),
```

- Role-Based Access Control (RBAC): Implementing RBAC at the application level allows finer-grained control over what operations users can perform.

6. Logging and Monitoring

Proactively monitoring your applications allows for the early detection of potential security issues. Logging valuable information while ensuring that sensitive data is not exposed in logs is essential.

- Centralized Logging: Using tools like Logstash, Kibana, or

Grafana to collect and visualize logs from distributed Erlang nodes.

- Audit Trails: Keeping detailed logs of access and operation events allows for auditing and tracking potential security incidents.

7. Dependency Management

Managing external dependencies securely ensures that you are not inadvertently introducing vulnerabilities into your system.

- Hex Package Manager: Regularly update dependencies and ensure that you are using secure versions of libraries.
- Source Verification: When possible, audit the source code of dependencies or use tools that can scan for known vulnerabilities.

Making security a priority in the development and deployment of Erlang applications will yield systems that are more resilient to attacks and failures, enhancing overall reliability. By combining these practices, developers can build and maintain robust and secure systems capable of meeting stringent security requirements.

10.9 Emerging Trends and Future Directions

Erlang, a functional, concurrent programming language, continues to evolve with advancements that solidify its relevance in modern computing environments. This section explores emerging trends and future directions in Erlang, focusing on both technical and community-driven developments. By examining these trends, readers can gain insights into how Erlang is adapting to contemporary challenges and innovations.

1. Integration with Modern Toolchains and Ecosystem: Many modern software projects leverage heterogeneous systems and toolchains. The Erlang ecosystem is expanding to include better integration with tools such as Docker, Kubernetes, and modern CI/CD pipelines. By leveraging these tools, Erlang applications can achieve better containerization, orchestration, and deployment flexibility. This makes deploying and managing Erlang systems in diverse environments simpler and more efficient.

```
docker build -t my_erlang_app .
docker run -d --name my_erlang_app_container my_erlang_app
```

The output of running the above Docker commands would show:

```
Successfully built <image_id>
Successfully tagged my_erlang_app:latest
<container_id>
```

2. Enhanced Support for WebAssembly (Wasm): WebAssembly is becoming a significant player for executing code on various environments efficiently. Erlang developers are exploring how to compile and run Erlang code within the Wasm runtime, enabling Erlang applications to run securely in browsers. Projects like WasmX are at the forefront, providing experimental support to this burgeoning area.

3. Improved Performance and Scalability: Performance optimizations remain a continuous effort within the Erlang community. Techniques such as Just-In-Time (JIT) compilation are being explored to enhance the performance of Erlang applications. Additionally, enhancements in garbage collection and scheduler improvements contribute to better scalability and reduced latency.

```
-module(optimization_demo).
-export([compute/1]).
compute(N) when N > 0 -> lists:sum(lists:seq(1, N)).
```

```
34> optimization_demo:compute(10).
55
```

4. Expanding Library and Framework Support: The ecosystem of libraries and frameworks around Erlang is expanding. Notable ones include the Elixir language, which runs on the Erlang VM and provides enhanced productivity for certain types of applications. Frameworks like Phoenix for web development, and Nervous for IoT applications, continue to bolster Erlang's practical applications.

5. Machine Learning and Data Analysis: While traditionally not a strong suit for Erlang, the rise of libraries like Erml, for machine learning, and ExPyPlot for data visualization in Elixir, indicate an increasing interest in data-heavy applications. These libraries facilitate the integration of Erlang with existing machine learning and data analysis tools, providing new avenues for its application.

6. Focus on Security Enhancements: Given the proliferation of cyber threats, security in distributed systems is of paramount importance. New security practices and tools are being introduced to fortify Erlang applications against vulnerabilities. These include better cryptographic libraries, improved standards compliance for secure communication (e.g., TLS 1.3), and enhanced capabilities in the ssl application for managing certificates and keys securely.

ssl:connect/3 function can be used to establish secure connections.

```
{ok, Socket} = ssl:connect("example.com", 443, [{verify, verify_peer}, {cacertfile, "/
    path/to/cacert.pem"}]).
```

The establishment of a secure SSL connection would typically output:

```
{ok, <ssl_socket>}
```

7. Extension to Cloud-Native Applications: As cloud-native architectures become more prevalent, Erlang's inherent strengths in building distributed and fault-tolerant systems align well with cloud paradigms. Emerging practices involve the use of Erlang in serverless computing models, seamless autoscaling using platform-native capabilities, and deploying resilient microservices architectures.

8. Community and Educational Initiatives: The growth of any programming language heavily relies on its community. The Erlang community is actively working on initiatives to make the language more accessible, such as improved documentation, online courses, and enhanced tooling for better development experience. Community conferences like Code BEAM foster knowledge sharing and innovation, keeping the ecosystem vibrant and forward-looking.

These trends collectively indicate that Erlang will continue to find new applications and enhancements, driven by both technological advancements and a dedicated community pushing for continuous improvement and relevance. By staying abreast of these trends, developers can better prepare for the future trajectories of Erlang and its place in the evolving landscape of programming languages.

Made in United States
Orlando, FL
04 November 2026

90201057R00134